COUNTRY
SKILLS
AND CRAFTS

COUNTRY
SKILLS
AND CRAFTS

*How to use, barter or sell
what you raise, grow and make*

Maureen Little and Craig Hughes

Spring Hill

Published by Spring Hill

Spring Hill is an imprint of How To Books Ltd
Spring Hill House, Spring Hill Road,
Begbroke, Oxford, OX5 1RX, United Kingdom
Tel: (01865) 375794 Fax: (01865) 379162
info@howtobooks.co.uk
www.howtobooks.co.uk

How To Books greatly reduce the carbon footprint of their books by sourcing their typesetting
and printing in the UK.

First edition 2011

British Library Cataloguing in Publication Data
A catalogue record for this book is available from the British Library

ISBN: 978 1 905862 67 2

Text illustrations by Firecatcher Creative
Produced for How To Books by Deer Park Productions, Tavistock
Typeset by TW Typesetting, Plymouth, Devon
Printed and bound in Great Britain by MPG Books Group, Bodmin, Cornwall

CONTENTS

PART 2   PLANTS

PART 3   FOOD AND DRINK

PART 4   CRAFTS

PART 5   PRACTICALITIES

ACKNOWLEDGEMENTS

We are both indebted to a number of people who have helped us, knowingly or unknowingly, in the writing of this book.

Our thanks go to our case study experts – Susan Carvell, Linda Clough, Hawky, Charlie Horn, Andrea Jones, Gill and Martin McManoman, Jekka McVicar, Gill Pateman, Teresinha Roberts, Martin and Kate Russell, Rose Shepherd, and Mike Woods – who either volunteered or were persuaded to allow themselves to be featured in this book: their input has been invaluable.

We also owe a huge debt of gratitude to Spring Hill Publishers, and especially Giles Lewis and Nikki Read.

And thanks, of course, to our respective families: especially to Georg, for his love, encouragement, assistance, and bars of Divine dark chocolate; and to Jacki for her support and help, and the cups of tea in the wee small hours.

Craig would also like to acknowledge:

My mother, who never understood what I did, was confused by everything I tried and was clearly excited by the first book I ever wrote. And who chooses the wrong milk for tea.

Joni Mitchell, whose songs and poetry have guided and aided my soul over 35 desperate and desert-like years, and has still to make me a cup of tea.

Gill Dempsey, who I betrayed and for which I am eternally sorry. And your lovely cups of PG tips.

INTRODUCTION

'. . . my nature is subdued
To what it works in, like the dyer's hand.'

Shakespeare, *Sonnet CXI*

'Jack of all trades, master of none
– though oftentimes better than master of one.'

Old saying

From time to time the fancy of many steers away from the tedium of cement-lined suburban or city life to the positively alluring, lush pastures of the countryside. We all reach that Sunday evening point of collapse: a 'feel-good' television programme about life in an English village in the nineteenth century has just finished; we look at the rain outside and wonder if the dogs can cross their legs until morning; and hope that the early morning crush into work won't be as bad as it normally is.

Most of us look towards the countryside for a glimpse of a reassuring past and a possible future. We look for pointers that will show us how to take steps to discover a slower, more graceful and relaxing approach towards life. And linked to that is the desire to find out more about the skills and crafts that, if not essential to such a lifestyle, are at least helpful in trying to turn our vision of a 'country life' into reality. Which is where this book comes in.

Craig: I have been living and working in the countryside for some time, but it was only after several years, and having preached for so long about my concerns over the countryside and its creatures, that I decided to leave the world of law and the constrictions of an office and 'put my money where my mouth is'. And I have become a 'Jack of all trades – master of none' as a result.

Maureen: And I am a 'Jill of all trades, mistress of none'! I always used to look on this term as rather derogatory – it is often used with a slightly condescending tone, edged with just a touch of disdain. Now I view it completely differently, probably because I feel it's an accurate description of what I am. Like Craig, I can turn my hand to a number of skills and crafts. I keep bees and have kept chickens; I grow herbs and flowers and have grown fruit; I can make jams and have tried making soap and dyeing. I can also keep accounts (I worked for an accountant for a number of years), and teach (I lectured at university). While I cannot claim to be an expert in any of those fields, I have enough knowledge and experience to make a reasonable and informed job of each. So I'm quite proud to be a Maureen of all trades – although in today's parlance we might be described as having a plethora of 'transferable skills'!

We would like to share some of our know-how with you, so we have gathered some of our 'transferable skills' together. And perhaps we should emphasize the bit of the saying that is often forgotten: 'Jack of all trades, master of none, *though oftentimes better than master of one.*' We couldn't agree more. You don't have to be a time-served expert in the skills and crafts we look at to gain pleasure and satisfaction from them. What is important is that you have an underlying desire to learn more and, at the same time, enjoy the experience.

The book is divided into four parts, each covering one group of skills or crafts that you might come across in your 'country life', whether or not you actually live in the country.

Craig has written Part 1 which covers keeping livestock – chickens, goats, and bees. He has a passion for all of these, although there is an extra twinkle in his eye when you mention bees!

Maureen takes over for Part 2 where you can get down and dirty with her, growing herbs, soft fruit, and flowers for cutting.

In Part 3 Craig takes us to the dairy and brewery, and Maureen into the kitchen, to look at how to make cheese, cider and mead, and sweet preserves, respectively.

In Part 4 Maureen examines soap making and works with some natural dyes, and Craig, wielding his toolbox and timber, joins Maureen to look at chicken coops.

At first glance you may think that the topics we have chosen have little, if anything in common, but as the chart shows, there is at least one link between each of them.

All the topics have this in common: you can either have a go at them simply for your own enjoyment and satisfaction, or you can regard them, or their 'by-products', as a commodity you can exchange or sell. You may not have the time or inclination to turn them into a part-time, or even full-time, money-spinning occupation, but in order to show you that this is actually possible we have included accounts from various case study experts, some of whom have done just that. What is obvious with each of them is that they are not in it solely for the money (although, of course, it has to be a consideration): what shines through is their love for their subject. Their passion for, and pride in, what they do become ingrained in their product.

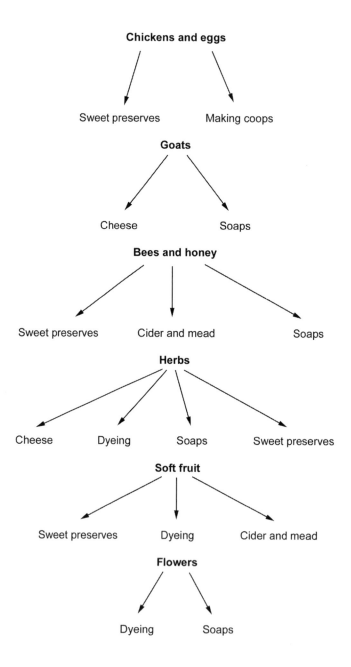

Part 5 contains two short chapters on the subjects of rules and regulations, and sharing and selling. These only really apply if you go down the route of exchanging or trading your product, which to some extent we have assumed you will. Information is given about who you need to contact, for example, and how you can go about selling your excess.

PART 1
Livestock

Introduction

In Part 1 we look at how to keep chickens, goats and bees. When you deal with animals, large or small, you will always feel the enthusiasm and delight of being the one who nurtures and cares for them and their well-being, and, from a practical point of view, makes the day-to-day decisions about them. You will decide where they are housed, what they are fed, and ultimately, how they will meet their end.

When you want a glass of milk it can come from your goats; your breakfast egg can come from your chickens; honey to spread on your toast can come from your bees. And there is a huge satisfaction to be gained from it. There is, of course, always a tinge of sadness when an animal has to be dispatched, but more often than not you make this choice – not the supermarket – and there is a degree of fulfilment in this too, because you know your animals have been looked after and cared for throughout their lives. And if all goes well, your produce may be sufficient to have enough left over to exchange with your neighbours or sell at a market.

CHAPTER 1

KEEPING CHICKENS

Over the years I have had experience of a number of activities concerning the garden and smallholding. I have kept bees and pigs and had great fun with a goat or two. Yet the one animal (other than the bees) I have always kept is chickens. I love their sociability: every time I go to collect the eggs or change their water they will come over to have a chat; after a while you can even pet them. I don't, however, give them names, and I advise other people to do likewise; it can be upsetting to know that the chicken on your plate was once called Henrietta, or that the fox has destroyed Bertie your favourite bantam. Nevertheless it is hard not to get attached to them. I still get excited when I look into the coop and find an egg, which I can take back to the kitchen to eat with soldiers and a big mug of tea.

CASE STUDY – MIKE WOODS

Mike Woods lives in Faversham. I've known Mike for a long time, and for much of that time he has been known to me as Gromit: with the lift of an eyebrow he looks like Wallace's famous doggy companion. Gromit has kept chickens for years. He has always had a selection of the most wondrous birds: different breeds, colours and sizes are always to be found under his feet, which in itself is surprising as Gromit has cerebral palsy and by his own admission struggles to walk in a straight line. He has great fun trying to catch his chickens, he tells me.

When I visited Gromit some years ago his flock had grown considerably. He had always had a collection of Orpingtons and Wellsummers, but they were now outnumbered by Warrens. Warrens are a beautiful hybrid bird, bred for their stamina, hardiness and egg-laying abilities. Many of Gromit's Warrens are former battery or barn stock. He pays 50p for each bird, takes them back to his holding, feeds them, fluffs them up, removes any mites and generally checks that they are healthy.

They are pretty helpless when they arrive: most don't know how to perch, or how to avoid getting stuck in a puddle. They have no idea about going indoors for the night; they would stay outside, some of them succumbing to the cold because they have so few feathers – they almost look like oven-ready birds.

Nor do they have an instinct about moving into the shade and out of the sun: Gromit came home from the supermarket one day in summer to find several of the featherless birds standing in the sun, obviously hot and distressed, becoming dehydrated. Gromit pulled out the first thing from his shopping that might alleviate their suffering: Greek yoghurt. He rubbed it on the birds and put them into the shade. He swears that from the looks on the birds' faces they were convinced that he was marinating them before putting them on a spit.

Gromit has always enjoyed his rare and unusual breeds and the coloured eggs you receive from some of them, but he was touched that these Warrens were to be despatched just because they were no longer laying enough eggs. A bird usually lays about 230 to 265 eggs a year, some more, some less. These Warrens were laying 365 eggs a year, and when they collapse as a result, that's that.

Gromit 're-educates' the hens and after about six weeks they are 'birds' again: they know how to peck and scratch, they are aware of foxes and sunshine and, more importantly, they lay when they want to. They are, as he says, Gromit's Happy Hens.

PREPARING THE GROUND

Placing your chicken coop

Like Gromit, you may like to keep chickens, and even give a home to rescued ones. Before you rush into things, you need to prepare the ground, literally. First you should identify where your coop is going to stand; ensure that the land is well drained, or at least that the coop isn't going to be sitting in water a lot of the time. Place your coop on bricks or, better, breeze blocks, to keep the coop right off the ground. Wrap some chicken wire around the base of the coop and bury a good portion of it in the soil. This will help to prevent any stoats, weasels or rats from nesting underneath or robbing from the coop.

Constructing a chicken run

Unless you want your chickens to wander free, you will need to fence them in. Stout posts supporting chicken wire is ideal. Your birds should be behind a fence at least 2 metres high, otherwise a fox will easily jump over. The bottom of the wire needs to be buried at least 30cm below ground and pinned down, otherwise a fox, stoat or weasel will burrow underneath. Occasionally rabbits, too, will burrow underneath and create a run: rabbits themselves are not harmful but their runs will allow all sorts of undesirables in. If you see a hole, always block it up.

There's a lot more about coops and runs in Chapter 10, so for now I'll move on.

Vermin and foxes

It doesn't matter how well you secure your coop and pen, unfortunately rats will always try to get in. They will squeeze through even the smallest hole if they detect a free meal. Not only will they take the chicken feed, they will also attack chicks, and sometimes even a hen.

The worst culprit, however, is the fox. Don't be under any delusions: foxes are not cuddly and cute, neither are they slightly uncivilized dogs. They are ruthless killers that will snatch a hen, attack a piglet and, as has been reported in the news, even a child. Make sure that you lock the birds in at night. A fox in the coop won't take just one bird, they will take one or two and kill the rest, just for fun so it appears. I've known people lose their whole livelihood because of an unlocked door, a hole in a fence or a forgotten latch.

A fox among poultry will circle the birds all the time, working itself into a frenzy. It will snap and lunge at the birds, who huddle together, though some will fly and try to escape. Or the fox will stare at the birds trying to pick out the weakest. Any elderly, infirm and or very young birds are likely to be caught. The majority of the birds will run together to a corner as far away from the fox as possible. Even if this means they are safe from the fox, as they crowd together they can suffocate themselves, or suffer heatstroke, and they die en masse. It's not a pretty sight.

Providing food and water

You must provide your birds with a feeder and a water bowl, changing the water every day. Make sure you remove the feed at night, otherwise rats will see this as a free meal. Gromit tells me that he had a family of rats actually living under his feeder. Also ensure that there is some dry ground for the birds to dust bathe in.

SETTLING IN YOUR STOCK

So now you have your well-secured pen, bright, airy coop, and supplies of fresh water and feed. When you have decided what you want from your livestock – are you rearing them for eggs or for meat? – then it's time to get some birds: this is the best part of the process. Go online first, and look at a number of sites. My favourite is www.chickenbreeds.info – it offers good advice and support.

Don't buy the first birds you like the look of: you might fall in love with them but then realize later that they are not suitable.

Another good way to get an idea of birds available and prices is to go to a poultry auction. There are many around the country, often held weekly, and you will see hundreds of birds, in singles, pairs and trios. A trio is two hens and a cock; a pair is always two hens; a single can be either/or. You might see a cock with prolific breeding powers or a hen with the genes of a supreme champion, but always take time to consider before you buy. If you can, take an experienced chicken keeper along with you – their advice will be invaluable.

CHOOSING YOUR BREED

I asked my friend Gromit about his choice of breeds. Before he went headlong into rescuing Warrens, his selection was mainly of ones he fancied. He had some beautiful Buff Orpingtons with their sandy yellow feathers, with Charlie the cock standing tall and proud. Charlie, like all other cocks, will defend his harem. Unfortunately this means that the cock might go for you as well.

Once an adolescent fox tried to get in to the hens. Before Gromit could rush to get his gun he heard a dreadful commotion and turned to see Charlie attacking the fox. The fox darted off, and when he went to check on the Buff Gromit found blood on the straw. But it wasn't from Charlie – he was unscathed – the blood was from the fox.

The following is a selection of breeds commonly found in smallholdings.

Orpington

These chickens are popular, friendly, easy to tame and will give a good number of large, brown eggs – around 200 – a year. Orpingtons can be a variety of colours: Black, Buff, White and Splash. Orpingtons look a lot heavier than they are because of the amount of feathers they have – which incidentally are good for pillows.

Sussex

The colours found in Sussex chickens are Brown, Buff, Light, Red, Speckled, Silver, White and Coronation. The variety of colours can be reason enough to have some, but they are also a lovely chicken. They give a light brown, medium egg at the rate of 240–260 a year. They are good foragers – you will never see a slug in your garden, but then you won't have much of a garden either. I have found that they are prone to turn broody very quickly, which is great if you want to expand your stock and need a sitter for your eggs, but not so good if you want a good layer.

Rhode Island Red

This hen is very popular throughout the world, especially in the UK. It's a beautiful bird, polite, alert and well mannered. A good all-rounder, it is ideal for both meat and eggs. The RIR lays the most beautiful medium to large deep brown egg. (Incidentally, it is sometimes thought that the browner the egg the better it is for you, this is not actually the case.)

A downside of the RIR is that they have a tendency to brood. They also prefer to be in the company of other birds of their own colour, namely reddish-brown; these birds will integrate with little problem with an existing group if they are all of a similar colour. So if you have RIRs or Warrens, you will find it easier to introduce another RIR or Warren into the flock than a Cotswold Legbar or a Lavender Araucana. RIRs are voracious eaters, too; don't leave too much food out as they will just eat and eat.

Wyandotte

Although seen as an American breed, the Wyandotte is well established throughout Europe and they come in a variety of colours and 'designs'. They are lovely to look at: the Lace Wyandotte is a most beautiful bird. The name comes from the delicate edges of the bird's feathers that look just like lace. It has a distinctive walk – it appears to shimmy. They are also incredibly friendly. If you want to introduce children to livestock, I would recommend the Wyandotte – they can stand any amount of hugging and petting, and produce up to 200 eggs a year.

Legbar

Gromit showed me these birds with pride and excitement. He told me that they are gentle, light, and a good all-rounder – dual-purpose birds. They lay the most beautiful green/blue eggs, about 200 a year.

BUYING YOUR BIRDS

Having selected your tribe, and before any money changes hands make sure that you are entirely happy with them. Have a look at their little legs. They should be a nice bright colour (either a pinky-white or yellow). Have a good look under their feathers or their armpits to check for lice and red mite. (I will talk about red mite later.) If you see any insects then the bird is infested and you must reject it. Too many red mites will cause anaemia and the bird will die quickly but painfully.

Transporting your birds

You need be equipped with a poultry crate or a well-ventilated cardboard box. Line the base of the crate or box with paper, as your new birds will relieve themselves en route. If you are transporting them any great distance – a journey of over 30 minutes, say – have some water in a sprayer with you and stop periodically to spray them to cool them down. Keep the windows open but not so much as to upset them – if they are upset, they will tell you in no uncertain terms!

On arrival

When you arrive back at base, get the chickens out of the crates and let them wander for a short time around the pen, supplied with food and water. When it is time for bed, place them in their coop with food and water and lock the door. Keep them in for at least 24 hours. When they are released they will identify the coop as their home; you may find that it takes them a while to venture outside. Make sure from the outset that you use clean straw and clean out the coop regularly. Scrape any waste off the perching rods regularly and check for any mite infestation.

Thereafter

You may find that although your birds may lay for the first day or two, they then suddenly stop. Don't worry about this. When birds have travelled, and have realized that they are no longer where they used to be, and feed and water are in a different place, they will slow down, almost going into shock. They will stop laying and may even lose their feathers, if they haven't lost them already. Be patient – they will begin to lay again.

HOW LONG DOES A CHICKEN LIVE?

A chicken can live for up to eight years, ten at a push. At about 18 months they begin to lay and will carry on laying an egg almost every day until they are about four years old. From then on they will lay an egg every other day or so until they are about six. At this stage you have to decide what is going to happen to your hen. Eating her will be hard-going both emotionally and because the flesh with be tough; but you will have no eggs and you may even have to help her up to her perch at night. Decision time.

BREEDING YOUR OWN STOCK

If you fancy having some lovely little chicks of your own, there are a few basic rules to follow. The idea of fluffy baby chicks tweeting around the garden sounds, and does look, lovely. Hatching your own chicks with a broody hen can be ideal, as the hen will have stopped laying anyway.

You will need a brood box and a run to isolate the hen in, as the problem with broody hens is that the other birds won't leave them alone. A brood box is essentially a large square wooden box with a lid, with lots of straw and plenty of water and food. The hen also needs enough protected space to walk and stretch her legs.

Gromit would build a six-foot run, either six feet square and placed over the brood box, or six feet long covering the brood box but giving no space around the back. The hen will come out from time to time, usually when no one is looking, to relieve herself and top up on food and water. The run needs to be weighted down and any holes blocked up: one year he lost all his chicks because a weasel managed to force itself through the tiniest of holes, killed all the chicks and then had a go at mum.

It's a good idea to place the 'broody run' close to a building where there is noise and movement, which acts as a deterrent to predators. Your broody hen should sit quite happily for 20–22 days, at which point the chicks will hatch.

'Abnormal' eggs and anomalies

You may find some smelly eggs among the clutch. These eggs have not been fertilized and will start to rot. Be careful when handling them, and if you have ever come across a rancid egg you will know what I mean. The sulphurous, sickening smell sticks to your hands and clothes and is difficult to remove.

When your broody hen has hatched out a number of eggs it often happens that she leaves the rest unattended. You can try to resit the hen back on the eggs, but if after a number of days she still isn't sitting, remove them. You may find that she probably knows better than you and there is something wrong with the eggs.

As she moves herself away from the eggs, remove any of the vacated shells because the sharp edges can damage the soft, newly hatched chicks. Don't be surprised if mum tries to peck you when you do this. Be patient with her, as she is only protecting her young.

Sometimes you find that eggs have been fertilized but are semi-developed; in this case, mum will always know. On one occasion, I picked out an egg that wasn't hatching, gently opened the shell, blew into the chick's mouth, clearing the airway, and dried it in my hand. Feeling very proud and elated, I wrapped the chick in a towel and put it on top of the Aga to dry completely. A couple of days later, fed on mash, and kept warm and snug, the chick was ready to go back to mum. When I presented her with junior, she attacked and killed the chick. A lesson learned: don't interfere with nature.

Penning

Give the chicks the opportunity to walk and run about and stretch their wings, but make sure they are protected from other hens. They won't look like 'Easter' chicks for long; they quickly look like small hens. After about six weeks of being penned up you could move them to another, larger pen closer to the older birds. This will help the youngsters integrate, and help mum to identify with the birds she left behind. Alternatively you may want to allow them to roam free; but they must have a place to run to in case they are picked on and pecked by the older birds.

Too many cocks

Your dilemma comes when you realize that you've raised a dozen chicks and 11 of them are cocks. If you keep them, you will probably have a permanent fight on your hands. As cocks mature they automatically establish a pecking order – literally. Some birds will be injured; others will take the hump and try to leave, taking members of the harem with them. And they will try to mate with as many hens as they can, which is not good news for the hens.

Or you can castrate the cocks, creating your own capons; they will wander around, not get into any trouble, and will still have a cock-a-doodle-do. This is a good option if you want to rear some fowl for the table.

A third option is to kill them and remove any cost of feeding.

Incubators

I have implied that interfering with nature is a bad thing, but sometimes you can give a helping hand. Gromit showed me a selection of his incubators – beautiful, scientific-looking machines, but apparently very simple to use. They keep the eggs at a constant temperature – as the hen would do – and at the correct humidity. They come in various sizes – some big machines can take thousands of eggs. Gromit tends to use ones that take around 20 to 30 eggs. Some have a floor vibrator unit, which gently rolls the eggs and stops the fluids within the egg from settling.

One machine recently on the market looks like a vibrating cushion or hot water bottle. The eggs sit comfortably underneath the cushion, which replicates mum's breast. A machine like this costs around £200. At the other end of the scale, you can buy a polystyrene one for as little as £30–£40, although in some cheaper ones it is difficult to regulate the temperature. If you buy a second-hand incubator, always clean it thoroughly before you use it.

DISEASES

Like any other form of livestock, chickens can catch diseases and be troubled by bugs. There are many chicken-related diseases and troubles that you will have to deal with, but the majority can be dealt with cheaply and conveniently. Listed here are the ones you are most likely to encounter.

Symptoms in general

The comb is a good indicator of a fault or problem. If it turns a bluish purple or greyish colour this usually indicates a blood-related problem. If the comb turns yellowish it may signify jaundice or liver disease. The other main indicator is the hen's excrement. A soft sulphurous green/grey colour with a white cap is good. If it's weak, diarrhoea-like, yellow or watery, then there is an issue with a virus or diet.

Avian flu or bird flu

There has been a lot of discussion about this virus over the years because of its ability to jump species. There are two categories of symptoms: severe and mild. Mild symptoms include ruffled feathers, a reduction in egg production, and minor respiratory issues such as sneezing – generally a bit off-colour. Sometimes the symptoms are so mild that you can have an outbreak and not even know it.

The more severe symptoms will be indicated by major respiratory issues, and a multiple organ failure which usually shows itself as a dull comb, watery waste and a lack of movement. The virus is spread in the secretions of the infected bird. You should take precautions against breathing in any air-borne secretions. Be aware that if you have a serious outbreak it could kill 100% of your birds within 48 hours.

If you think you have an outbreak or even if you are not sure, you should speak to your vet straight away as this is a notifiable disease.

Botulism

Botulism is a bacterial infection. It's quite difficult at times to detect but at its worst it can cause paralysis in the bird. It is generally contracted through the bird eating grubs and insects that already have the toxin in them.

Red mite

Red mites are actually grey, but they like to feed on the bird's blood around twilight when the sun sets. It's not easy to catch the red mite in action, as it were, and it's very hard to get rid of entirely, but you can stay on top of it. There is a specially formulated ammonia-based liquid cleaner that zaps the red mite. The mites love dark, quiet corners to skulk away into, so when you change the straw in the nesting boxes, spray the corners and edges of the boxes with the cleaner.

Another good piece of advice is to dust your birds with an organic lice and flea powder when you bed them down on their first night. You do this by grabbing the bird by its legs and turning it upside down: don't worry if it flaps and shouts, it will soon calm down. When it has settled, dust the bird liberally with the powder all over – under its wings, near its bottom and on the back of its neck. Repeat this treatment every six weeks. Try to avoid breathing in the powder, so wear a mask.

Coccidiosis

Coccidia is a parasite that lives in the intestines. It can be spread very easily. Don't think it's bad husbandry, it's just very common. You can generally tell if your birds have it because you will find bloody and/or watery stools. The parasite causes a scarring of the intestinal wall, which distresses the bird and can be fatal. Coccidia can live outside the body of a bird for a long time, so reinfection can happen when a brood pen or cage is reused. Always, therefore, be scrupulous about scrubbing out pens and cages before you use them again.

It is very difficult, if not impossible, to prevent coccidia, but it can be controlled with a drug, Coccidiostat, which you add to the feed. You can use the same drug in a vaccine but this will be expensive unless you are looking at a large commercial operation.

You might find that after an outbreak your flock will build up a resistance to that type of parasite; unfortunately, however, there are other strains that may take hold.

Gapeworms

Birds with gapeworms will stretch their necks as if they are yawning and then look like they are going to vomit. This condition causes minor discomfort which the birds can sometimes live with, but it can hamper their digestion. There is a very simple remedy, which is to add cider vinegar to their water. The vinegar causes the worms to reduce in size and then they are ejected in the stool.

Scaly leg

Scaly leg is commonly caused by burrowing mites. There is pitting, scale, or a crust-like development on the leg, or even a swelling of the tissue or loose, flaking flesh. You need to treat the condition, or there could be permanent disfigurement to the scaly areas. You can use products available from your vet, such as SCATT or Ivermectin.

You can also treat it successfully yourself, by applying petroleum jelly, benzyl benzoate or paraffin, which essentially suffocates the mites. (Gromit warned me against a product called Clarins – using his wife's handcream on scaly leg mite tended to result in a thick ear.)

Egg bound

I imagine being egg bound is a bit like having terrible constipation. It is caused mainly by low calcium levels, which can be corrected by feeding a supplement containing calcium and vitamin D. Alternatively, you can add finely crushed, boiled eggshells to the feed, and offer an open area in full sunlight to provide vitamin D. Other causes include malnutrition or not enough exercise, but if you provide your hens with good-quality feed and a large enough area to roam, these should not be a problem.

SELLING YOUR EGGS

Let's assume that your chickens are happy and are producing eggs. Remember that just four hens will produce about two dozen eggs a week over the laying period – all well and good if you like eggs for your breakfast every day, omelettes for lunch, or if you make lots of cakes. What happens if you have more hens – and even more eggs? You can extend your repertoire into quiches and egg custards – or you could sell the excess.

The easiest way of selling is at your gate, although if you go into hens in a big way then you will need other outlets. There are legal regulations that apply to all methods of selling eggs – look at the DEFRA website for more information (www.defra.gov.uk).

You might be able to offer a particular selling point. For example, if you have a selection of chicken breeds you will get eggs with shells of different colours. A large supermarket in England sells a variety of coloured eggs at twice the price of brown ones. Now the cost of producing a coloured egg is exactly the same as producing a brown one, and they taste exactly the same, but people are willing to pay a premium for something different – you get my drift.

CHAPTER 2

KEEPING GOATS

I always used to wonder why people would even consider keeping a goat. Having a pet in the house and looking after it as part of the extended family is different – I can understand that; I have three dogs and a cat. But I could never see the point of making pets of livestock, as all my animals were destined for the plate. Those were the rules, no matter how cute they were; the end result would be a tasty meal and/or the addition of a modest amount to my annual income.

Until I got pigs, that is – then I would sit up all night when the sows were pregnant; on one occasion I was found by a friend, reading Auden's poetry to a sow struggling to give birth. I wept when I returned the next day to find that she had rolled on them and squashed them all. So now I am not surprised that people become emotionally attached to their livestock – even if it is a goat!

CASE STUDY – GILL AND MARTIN MCMANOMAN

Gill and Martin McManoman of Capra Products in Lancashire rear goats for the food service industry. They farm over 200 head of goat (some of which have names, which really surprised me).

I had thought of them (the goats, that is) as slightly smelly, inquisitive lawnmowers, but I could see that this was the wrong thing to say to Gill as she clearly loves her animals, one and all. The couple use and sell a variety of goods that are a direct or indirect product of their 'extended family', as Gill calls them: everything from hard and soft cheese to diced meat, to angora. Gill showed off the jumper she was wearing; she explained that it had been made from the fleece of one of her goats, Charlie.

Gill gave me some very interesting advice about goats. She told me to remember that goats are *not* lawnmowers. Many people buy a goat thinking that they will happily munch away at the grass, keeping it nice and neat. But this is not how they graze, and she gets visibly upset when she tells me that thousands of goats are left to fend for themselves simply because people don't know, and haven't bothered to find out, how to keep them. Many end up being passed on to goat sanctuaries.

FEEDING YOUR GOATS

Is it true that they will eat anything and everything? They are inquisitive, it's true, and will have a nibble at anything out of curiosity. But they would much rather eat proper, suitable food than try to sustain themselves by eating rubbish. If they are denied appropriate food then they will eat things that you don't want them to eat, and that usually results in a visit from the veterinary.

Even hedgerow greenery can be bad for them, so if your goat's paddock is surrounded by a hedge it might be a good idea to erect an additional fence to keep them from browsing – unless, of course, you know exactly what is growing in it. Worst of all is the stuff the general public try to feed them. This is only likely to be a problem if your goat paddock backs on to a public footpath or the like, in which case consider putting up a sign asking them (the public) not to feed them (the goats).

Goats especially like good-quality hay, which fortunately is fairly easy to get hold of. You should feed your herd hay all year long and especially in winter when grazing is difficult. Goats like to feed standing up, so place your feed in a rack. If you use a net they will inevitably pull it down, eat their way through the nylon mesh and/or get their horns/stumps caught in the netting and rip the bag apart. They are not terribly clever – cute, but not clever. They also like good clean barley or oat straw, if you can get hold of it: it adds some variety to their dry diet.

As well as hay, goats like some green stuff such as apples, carrots, cabbages and the like. You could investigate whether your local supermarket, independent greengrocer, wholesaler or farm shop would consider passing your way any fruit and vegetables that are to be thrown away. If you explain what it is for and assure them that you will not be selling it on, nine times out of ten you can strike a bargain. If you think it through logically, everyone wins: the shop can feel that they are helping the environment, so it boosts their PR, and they don't have to pay for the surplus to be disposed of.

In the past I have been offered acres (literally) of organically grown cabbages for my pigs because it wasn't worth the farmer's while to harvest them. I was also offered a skip full of Chinese onions once – apparently they were too big! So it is possible to get a free lunch for your animals, and recycle foods that would otherwise be landfilled. An extra bonus of free food is the free goat manure you get, which you can use for growing your own vegetables, fruit or flowers. It can also be used to barter for other goods (more on bartering in Chapter 14).

It's a good idea to give your goats a supplement specially formulated for them. This will add to your goat's diet the minerals and trace elements that may not be present in other foodstuffs. Think of it as multivitamins for goats. There are different ones available; what you give them will depend on what you are rearing the goat for: milk or meat? Or you may be interested in developing stock, in which case the goat will be in kid a number of times.

Always have a mineral block in the yard for the goats to lick at, too. They will use it if they need to.

Goats need a regular source of clean water. You could install a trough with a ballcock on it but Gill warns me that horned goats will wreck them and those without horns are still far too curious for their own good. So change the water manually, or use a large circular feeder.

PROVIDING SHELTER

Goats are not like sheep, in that a goat's coat is not waterproof, like a sheep's fleece. Goats need a waterproof shelter for the majority of the time and access to a dry environment with clean, dry straw. Gill explained that when they started out they did not have state-of-the-art housing for their goat family so they used old caravans and an old livestock trailer. Now they have an all-singing, all-dancing unit but their improvised shelters served their purpose – it kept their animals dry and free from draughts, especially during the winter; and they were big enough for the goats to have plenty of space to move and jump about.

Make sure that your goat shelter is sturdy. They will rub themselves against the sides of the shelter and easily demolish it if it is too flimsy. As a rough guide, you will need an area about 10 square feet per pair of goats.

Be aware of where you put their shelter. Try to make sure it is in or next to their pasture so that they can get to and from it when the weather changes.

As well as having a dry, draught-free house, they need equally dry bedding. This means that they have to be mucked out regularly and the straw needs to be renewed.

If you can, lock up your herd at night to keep any unwanted visitors, such as foxes, at bay: they will readily snatch a kid given half the chance. A security light on a motion sensor is also a good idea.

KEEPING HAPPY GOATS

Goats will tell you when they are unhappy: they will bleat and will carry on bleating. Gill reckons that she can tell when some of them want a cuddle or a scratch. Whether or not it's true is a moot point, but Gill maintains that by giving her goats a good quality of life she gets a better product.

Goats are herd animals

Goats need company, so you will need to keep a minimum of two, or if this is not possible you can keep your goat with other animals, such as sheep, perhaps, or a cow; but they are terribly sociable creatures and will fret if they feel lonely. They will always be pleased to see you, and are likely to rush to greet you; they are really not keen on being isolated. So unless you want to move in with your goat, have a pair!

Goats are a commitment

Goats need daily attention, even if you are having them just as pets. It's a 365-day obligation, whatever the weather. If your routine includes regular trips away then you will need to get someone in every day to see to them – do you have patient friends with a good field knowledge of goats?

Check with your local veterinary practice to see whether they offer a service that includes goats, or have any specialist knowledge in these creatures. This is vitally important as a small animal practice may struggle to help you.

Intruders beware!

Goats make fantastic security guards. If they are awoken before they are ready there will be mass bleating in seconds: one starts and the rest kick off in chorus. If you've a problem with foxes or badgers, the goat will let you know when one is near, especially if there are any young around. Foxes tend to be drawn to the smell of the afterbirth and stale blood, so remove promptly any debris of this type into a sealed container.

Don't tether

I would guess that many people have the idea that a goat should be tethered – memories linger of Ladybird Books showing 'A Day in the Life of a Romany' with the image of a goat tethered to a rope, nibbling politely on some grass. It is actually very poor practice; it is frustrating for the animal, and poses a risk of injury because it can become entangled in the rope. If no one is around to untie it, it might strangle itself. It is also left to the mercy of the weather as it won't be able to move to find shelter, and as we know, goats don't have an in-built raincoat.

DISEASES

Like all animals, goats can catch a variety of diseases. One of the first signs that a goat is suffering is that it will go off its food. Normally goats like eating, so this is a sure indication that something is amiss. In addition, if a goat is being isolated by other goats – the goat may be standing alone, perhaps in an odd position, in a corner or in the middle of an open space – then investigate immediately. Isolate it, call the vet out and monitor it. If it is being 'sent to Coventry' by its mates then they are already aware of something wrong that may not be apparent to you. Animals often know when they are not long for this world and their chums know it as well.

Worms

Most animals appear to be at the mercy of some kind of worm or another. Worming should be carried out at least twice a year; the vet will do it, or you can do it yourself once you are confident. The symptoms of worms are diarrhoea, dehydration, rapid weight loss and kidney failure. You must keep on top of the worming regime to ensure a healthy goat. Be advised by your vet as to the best formulation and dosage.

Clostridial

Goats can suffer from clostridial disease. This is a stomach upset that produces toxins in the goat's body, giving diarrhoea often with mucus or blood in the waste. In very severe cases there is rapid weight loss and sudden death. Ensure that your goats have a well-balanced diet and are vaccinated every six months. Keep records of all the vaccinations for DEFRA.

Skin diseases

Lice, mange, ringworm and orf (a viral infection) are all common skin conditions in goats, and you need to check them regularly to ensure that they are free from these complaints. It is important to remember that you too can catch many of the same skin diseases, so be vigilant. Always wear disposable plastic gloves when dealing with an animal that is under the weather, or when giving medicines.

Caprine arthritic encephalitis or CAE

CAE is a virus that affects goats in multiple ways. It most often manifests itself in swollen knees, but can also do irreparable damage to the lungs; it affects the immune system, leaving the goat defenceless against common ailments. Goats can be treated against CAE – only ever buy stock from a breeder that can show you a negative CAE certificate. You will find that goats that have not been treated are not allowed to be shown; and no breeder will allow your untreated goats to breed with theirs. The problem is usually transmitted through contaminated milk given to a kid, or through the passing of bodily fluids.

Foot health

Ah, the joys of foot-trimming. It's not too bad if you have a steady hand and a steady goat – a piece of cake! Not so when it's raining, you have a subject with a hoof infection that smells and it won't keep still. Foot-trimming must be done approximately every six to eight weeks: the frequency will depend on various factors – the goat's age, its rate of growth, and its environment. It's a fairly straightforward process – a bit like cutting toenails, only bigger and tougher. You need to ask someone to show you how to do this at first – a goat-keeping friend or your veterinary – because an overenthusiastic foot trim can cause bleeding and great pain to the goat.

ARE YOU SURE YOU WANT A GOAT?

You need to think about what you want your goat for. I always assumed people had them for their milk, but there are other ways of using the animal. You should decide what your requirements are, and how committed you are.

Goats for milk

Let's say that you want a goat for milk. You need a nanny that will be put into kid yearly, or at least every other year, to ensure a good supply of milk. When she gives birth (probably at 2 a.m. in late winter) and when you take the kid away (yes, you have to if you want milk), mum will need milking twice a day, every day. This is a huge commitment so think carefully before you take it on.

Goats as pets

If you've decided that you want a goat just for the sake of it, you have a number of alternatives. You can buy a billy goat and have him castrated; this makes him docile, but he will also put on weight. One good thing about a castrated male is that the strong musky smell characteristic of an uncastrated male disappears.

Billy goats are ten a penny and you will probably be giving a home to an animal that would otherwise be destroyed. Remember the kid taken away from its mum? If it was a nanny then you could sell her for a reasonable sum, for breeding or milking. A billy would probably end up at the abattoir, unless he is taken as a pet.

Debudding

It is important that when they arrive with you your goats have been debudded, or dehorned. This will make your life, and the goat's life, a lot easier. It should be done when the horns are mere buds, so they are easy for the vet to remove. Removing horns from a mature goat causes unnecessary suffering.

Why remove them? Anyone who is butted by a goat will know about it and may be injured, especially children, and the blame will likely rest with you. It is probably best to avoid any problem of this type from the start.

Have you changed your mind?

If you still think you fancy keeping a goat (I should say two), then good; let's look now at some different breeds of goats.

CHOOSING A BREED

Cross-breeds as pets

A cross-breed might be a good choice if you are looking for a goat as a pet. I've always found that the mongrels of breeds are the hardiest, whether it's chickens, pigs or dogs. A top thoroughbred Afghan, for example, may be a show winner, but can be prone to dodgy hips and arthritis, whereas border collies are hard workers and live to a grand old age. It's much the same with goats.

Goats for milk

FRENCH ALPINE

The French Alpine is a sweet goat, and as its name suggests, originally from the Alps. They are multicoloured and no two are the same. They are excellent all-rounders: short-haired, with a high top average milk yield.

ANGLO NUBIAN

This is the most common and easily available breed. There is a wide variety of colours, sizes and shapes, but all are easily identified by the large Roman nose and long, lop ears. They are hardy, stout and determined. If you want a good milker this is your best choice, as it offers one of the highest butter fat contents. Remember that goats are noisy creatures and the Nubian is no exception; and unless you keep it with another goat it will cry non-stop – as mentioned earlier, goats hate being on their own.

SAANEN

The Saanen (pronounced Sah-nen) is a large, white beast with erect ears, and is heavy on milk production. They like a lot of shade, and will spend much time lying down relaxing in it.

TOGGENBURG

The brown and white Toggenburg is the oldest known breed; it's slightly smaller than the Alpine and has short to medium hair length. They have a pronounced pair of white stripes on each side of their face, and white on either side of their tail and a white rump. They are beautiful creatures – the Cindy Crawford of the goat world.

PYGMY GOATS

The African and Nigerian pygmy goats are lovely creatures which give a surprising amount of milk for their size. If you just want a couple of gallons of milk a week from a family goat then a dwarf breed could be your answer. They are good for meat, too, but not really viable for commercial purposes – the public would not pay the price you would need to get for them. Note that you will need to use a different fence gauge – pygmy goats will escape through a standard fence gauge.

ANGORA

Angora goats have curly coats and give fine milk. The La Mancha is a fine breed: it is sweet-tempered, inquisitive and a good milker. They look very different from other goats as they appear to have no ears.

OTHER BREEDS FOR MILKING

The Oberhasli has a red bay coat with a black face and feet, and they produce lovely, slightly sweet milk. Then there is the beautiful, but smaller, Golden Guernsey. These are a fine goat with a beautiful golden coat, lovely temperament and little feet.

Goats for meat

Gill and Martin farm Boer goats for meat production; they are a good, strong goat that are quick to bulk out, putting on a good amount of meat with just enough fat to baste their own flesh; they are not so good for milk. And they adapt well to variations in climate.

All goats have their pros and cons; for the Boer top of the cons is their ability to escape. To this breed a fence is like a hurdle to an Olympic athlete – it's there to be jumped.

UNDERSTANDING REGULATIONS AND RESTRICTIONS

Before you start

Once you have decided to go ahead, before you start talking to breeders and feed suppliers, and erecting your fence, you will need to contact DEFRA to obtain what is called a holding number and a flock number. This allows the Department to track any animal, through the flock number, when it is sold, moved or sent to slaughter. This helps with the isolation of disease outbreaks, scares and potential culling issues. It actually applies to all livestock, not just goats.

Your holding number is unique to your farm or smallholding, and is usually accepted for land up to three or four miles away from your given address. If it is further away than this, the field in which you keep the animals takes a different number. You can't transfer the number from farm to farm; you are issued with a new one when you move.

Movement restrictions

All cloven-hoofed animals are subject to strict movement regulations in the UK and Europe: goats, sheep, pigs and deer are all covered by this category. Since the last foot and mouth disease outbreak, cloven-hoofed animals require a movement licence when they are transferred from one site to another. This doesn't necessarily mean from one field or housing section to another, but certainly between farms for, say, breeding purposes, or to the abattoir, or for sale.

If you intend to buy an animal that has to be transported more than 60 miles then you must have a transportation licence. This can be obtained by doing a short, approved course; DEFRA will have details of where these sessions are held – usually your local agricultural college.

ANIMAL IDENTIFICATION AND THE MOVEMENT BOOK

Every animal you buy, with the exception of poultry, needs to have identification in the form of an ear tag or tattoo. Never buy an animal without proper identification. That number has to be displayed, and is recorded in your animal movement book.

The movement book is your responsibility and needs to be kept up to date for inspection at any time. DEFRA are legally allowed to visit you to look at your documentation without giving notice; normally, however, they write to you, providing a series of possible dates and times. In my experience I have never known them to drop in unannounced; remember, they are there to help you, not to try and catch you out.

Even if you have only one goat – even a tiny pygmy goat – in the eyes of the law this constitutes a herd. If your pet goat is unregistered or untagged your life will become very difficult. Think about this scenario. You have a small herd of goats that you rely on for your (modest) income; you and your spouse or partner have left secure jobs to become farmers; everything is ticking over nicely. What you don't know is that someone close by, say within a three-mile radius, has a little pygmy goat as a pet. It isn't registered or numbered, and is infected with foot and mouth. The goat dies and the disease is spread. Even though your herd is loved, secured, healthy, and most of all disease-free, you will lose them all. Your livelihood is gone, and there is a standstill order for you and your family not to move off the farm. All because of an unregistered goat.

As from 2010 the deaths of all goats aged 18 months or more have to be reported to DEFRA. If you are in any doubt, look on their website (www.defra.gov.uk) or call them (freephone 0800 25890, seven days a week) and ask for the Animal Welfare Department. I have always found that they would rather be bothered and it be a mistake, than not.

HOW TO GET YOUR GOAT

If you are wise, you will have done your preparation before your new arrivals appear – everything we have spoken about and more – so you will be able to bring your goats straight into their new surroundings. If you use something makeshift – an old shed, perhaps – at the beginning, when you do come round to providing proper surroundings you will confuse the goats and have trouble retraining them into where they live.

There may be someone local you can buy your goats from. If not, I suggest looking in one of the very good smallholder magazines. They often have articles and advertisements specially designed for people looking to get started in smallholding.

You can also explore the internet, or contact a local goat society or rescue centre – although the goats at rescue centres are sometimes there because they are troublesome. Try contacting the British Goat Society (details at the end of the book), which has a list of breeders and is happy to advise. Or you could contact a local agricultural society and ask them for a list of exhibitors.

Remember that buying livestock is no different from any other 'commodity' – you get what you pay for, so the offer that appears too good to be true probably is just that.

CHAPTER 3

KEEPING BEES

Many people are keen to keep bees these days; you may have already made up your mind to do so. For some it is for the pleasure of knowing that they are helping the environment and supporting society as a whole. They recognize that bee keeping is in trouble, stocks are in decline and diseases and mites are prevalent. It is these bee keepers that I take my hat off to. They are not looking to improve their bank balances but act for the greater good.

You might also be interested that keeping a few colonies will enhance the productivity of your own flowers, fruit and vegetables. A little-known fact is that per acre, a hive can improve productivity by 18% guaranteed, and up to 36% if the conditions are right. So if you are a smallholder with a couple of acres, a hive may very well be a move in the right direction.

I would hazard a guess, however, that the majority of you relish the idea of having sweet, sticky honey on your breakfast porridge or tea-time toasted crumpet.

TYPES OF HONEY

Polyflora honey

If your bees are feeding on a variety of flowers then the honey will reflect that assortment – bees fly up to three miles to forage for pollen and nectar (but will stay much closer to the hive if they can), so you will undoubtedly get a 'polyflora' honey from your bees. If your hive is placed at the bottom of a garden, on a flat roof, at an allotment or in a secluded spot in a park, your honey will be a mixture of what is available close by.

Town honey

In town environments you will also get a mixed honey. We have experimented with urban bee keeping, placing hives in parks in Manchester, on rooftops (an old pub roof in Liverpool and an inner-city council rooftop in Blackpool), and in a disused factory car park close to a canal in Birmingham. The bees produced amazing honey, full of flavour, showing that they had found a variety of nectar in what at first glance were barren areas.

Some of the best honey I've ever tasted came from inner-city areas of Paris, Hamburg and Boston. And if you are ever walking down Piccadilly in London, look up and you might see hives on hotel roofs, supplying the hotels with their own honey.

Bees in the parks in Manchester feed on clover, broadleaf trees and fruit trees, and flowers planted up in beds, which will vary at different times of the year. Bees placed near sycamore trees produce a beautiful dark honey from the nectar collected, almost like molasses. (You might think that a dark honey affects the colour of the wax, but this is not so.)

Heather honey

If you are fortunate to live near high ground you might have the opportunity to take your bees for an outing to the moors to work the heather. Heather honey has antiseptic qualities (as effective as manuka), and tastes really good. It has always been the Rolls Royce of the honey world: thick, with a caramel, toffee flavour. It's lovely to cook with and equally delicious in a good whisky or cognac!

WHAT YOU CAN LEARN FROM POLLEN

You may be able to identify what the bees have been feeding on by the colour of the pollen. A pollen chart, available from bee-keeping suppliers or online, helps you to sort out the different colours. The majority of pollen is yellow or orange but you might find the odd deep blue or burgundy: they will be poppy and dead nettle respectively.

If you leave your hive in one place for the year, when you remove your honey at the end of the season you will see the different colours of pollen, showing the places where the bees have been and the distance they have travelled – all the hard work they have carried out to produce this marvellous sticky harvest.

OTHER BEE PRODUCTS

Uses of honey

Bees are kept to produce honey for other uses too. You may see it as a business opportunity to use honey as an ingredient in another product. For example, you can use honey in cosmetics, such as creams, balms and soaps (Linda Clough, our soap expert in Chapter 11, uses it in one of her soaps), or you can make mead or braggot (more on that in Chapter 9). And the wax can be used to make polish or candles – but that will have to wait for another book!

Propolis

There is a growing interest in the propolis that bees make. Propolis is what bee keepers refer to as 'bee glue'. It is a substance that the bees create from tree resin and a secretion, and they use it to block up holes or support weak areas that might be allowing vibration to disturb the colony's peace and quiet. Bees will use propolis, rather than wax, to shore up any fissures that allow draughts of cold air in or heat to escape.

But it's not just used as an adhesive by bees; many people recognize its health-giving qualities and use it for a variety of medicinal treatments. I knew one chap who vowed that taking propolis, mixed with neat whisky, kept his blood pressure down and his digestion in order. Propolis production can be made into a (ignore the pun) healthy business.

FIRST THINGS FIRST

Having decided to keep bees, there are a few things you need to do first. One is to read a book on bee keeping (see those listed at the end of the book); another is to get stung; another is to look at the deeds of your property to see whether you are allowed to keep bees in your garden. It's important to find this out before you spend a lot of money needlessly.

If you say that you have decided to keep bees you will get no end of advice from a multitude of people, particularly about choosing the right 'variety' of bee and the right hive for your environment. Don't take what they tell you as gospel. I was told that polystyrene hives were dreadful, that wood was the best, that one particular type of bee was better than another, and so on. Forget it. Traditionalists believe that all hives should be made of wood, and so 'look like a hive', whereas I have become a convert to the polystyrene variety.

If it's all systems go, and you can gather enough information to identify what kind of hive and bees you need for your purpose, you can move in the correct direction.

CHOOSING A HIVE

There is, however, nothing wrong with wooden hives. The traditional WBC (the one everyone recognizes as a beehive) looks great in a garden, but they are draughty, heavy and expensive and have a life of only around 25 years. They need painting every year and are incredibly heavy if you decide to move the colony to another site.

Other hives, like the National, Dadant or Smith, follow a similar design in that they are wooden and single stack, but they look less traditional because they don't have the tiered outline of the WBC.

When placing your hive, either hide it out of sight from the public or place it in full view, advertising what it is; these are the preferable options as it is less likely to be stolen. Leaving it just a little in view will lead to curiosity from passers-by who may be tempted to come and look, poke around, get stung and then try to blame you for their stupidity.

CASE STUDY – CRAIG HUGHES

For this chapter I feel that I am the best person to make a case study of. I started keeping bees at secondary school. I was invited to do so by a teacher; I think he quite fancied the idea of seeing me, the school geek, getting stung repeatedly. It was the start of a love affair with the bee. I fell in love with all of them – every single one. And I am still in love with them.

For the years I was in full-time work I always kept hives, ranging in number from one to 20. I would rush home from work like a schoolboy released early from class, then hurry along the motorway to reach the hives and examine them. But after a bout of life-threatening illness I decided to move away from my previous profession to try my hand at keeping bees on a commercial basis.

I was very surprised how different it was to keep several hundred hives rather than just a couple. I know what you are thinking: of course it would be different. But the difference wasn't the number of bees, nor was it the amount of honey: it was the coordination of the whole thing.

Amateur to professional

I had become a farmer, not just an amateur with a bee-love affair. The logistics of this became massive. When you have just one or two hives in your back garden, they function as they are supposed to do: the bees pollinate flowers and make honey. But when you multiply that by 200, you suddenly realize the logistics of merely finding enough food for the bees to forage on. You need to work on the basis of one to one: one hive to one acre. So you have to find enough forage for 200 hives – quite a monumental task.

Persuading the farmers

It wasn't so much that there weren't enough crops to pollinate, it was more the fact that farmers immediately kicked against the opportunity of having bees on their land. They were worried about the public wandering off the footpaths and being stung. Economics always gets the upper hand, though, and once I had explained that I could increase their crop yields by a guaranteed 18%, they became interested.

But it was incredibly difficult to get to see them in the first place. It took me a good 12 months to win the confidence of the farming community, and after another 12 months, as the improvements in yield were noted, I was able to persuade the farmers to plant crops that would keep the bees in forage over a full season, which in turn influenced how often I had to move the hives, or in this case, didn't have to. Bees don't like to be moved too much. My bees are moved now only when they are taken to the heather up on the moors, and then back to their over-wintering sites.

The logistics of moving hives

Before turning professional I had not given any thought to moving 200 hives, let alone the logistics of such an undertaking. In the past I had left the bees where they were, the only considerations being, could I gain access easily, was the hive a danger to the public, and could I move it at a moment's notice if I had to.

The crunch came when I wanted to move the hives to the heather. I already had a good pick-up, but it only took about ten hives. So I bought a big trailer that took 30. But when I got to the moors I realized that I could not get the pick-up and the trailer up the tracks to get the bees right among the heather, where they would do best. So I bought an ex-army Bedford 4 × 4 which comfortably took 150 hives and went anywhere, but at only three miles to the gallon. Thus the cost of getting to the heather began to outweigh the profits I could make. I am not trying to put you off, just illustrating my foolish lack of preparation.

Joining a bee-keeping society

I had joined one or two bee-keeping societies with the idea that they would be able to point me in the right direction concerning stock and materials. After a short time I realized that I had learned all I needed to from the local bee keepers because what they wanted from me was to be as traditional as they were. People who keep bees often have established views, but for the craft/practice to survive it needs people who are willing to escape from the 'traditional' vision of the middle-class, semi-retired professional who keeps a hive at the bottom of a cottage garden.

Types of hives

I started to use polystyrene Langstroth hives initially because other bee keepers told me not to – I've always had a stubborn streak. I found that they are the most popular hive in the world, and the bees like them. Being made from non-organic material, they do not attract a high level of disease.

That's not to say I have not had an issue with disease. I once had American foul brood, and three hives had to be destroyed, bees and all. I cried because I had let my livestock down. I am a commercial bee keeper with several hundred hives, but even those three upset me. I can still hear the noise they made when I poured petrol on them.

As well as being better from a disease point of view, poly hives are easy to move, easy to clean, and don't break easily. Like any hive, though, they need to be secured with a weight to stop them blowing over in strong winds. And while this may seldom happen in the late spring and summer, you will have to secure them for the winter.

Other wildlife

In the spring, as the bee community starts to ready itself for the next season, other wildlife starts to be active too. You might find that Mr and Mrs Woodpecker love nothing better than perching on the side of a wooden hive and annoying the bees. They will break into hives, not for the contents but in the mistaken belief that it might make a good home for their forthcoming family. They don't do this with polystyrene.

Rats and mice may gnaw on the side of the hive, break in and rob the honey and wax. Mice, especially, will break in, have a snack and settle down for the winter. I have come across a variety of rodent life secreted around hives. I once found a mouse wrapped in wax in a poly hive; on another occasion, a rat had eaten its way through the wall, but the polystyrene balls it had ingested started to swell inside its gut and killed it. Because the rat's head was on the inside and a slight draught had been created, the colony had covered its head in wax and the sides in propolis!

If you are unfortunate enough to have a hive destroyed by a badger or a deer, there is little you can do. I watched once as a badger took a poly hive apart in around three seconds – it wasn't bothered by the bees who were obviously upset by this intrusion. It took some honey on the comb and casually walked away. The only difference in this case between a poly hive and a wooden hive is that poly hives are cheaper to replace.

As for deer, I was helping a friend move hives in the Angus region of Scotland when we noticed a young deer rubbing its antlers against a hive. The deer knocked over the hive and was promptly covered in bees. It ran off, shaking its head and antlers, only to reappear five minutes later to have a second go at the hive, which it destroyed. Not the brightest of creatures. But take heart – you shouldn't get these problems if you live in a town or city.

CHOOSING YOUR BEES

Choosing a queen

The first thing you have to do is choose a queen. The queen has to be accepted by the rest of the colony, and having a queen accepted isn't a sure fact – sometimes things go wrong and the queen is ignored, damaged or killed.

Getting a colony balanced is dependent on the queen, the stock (bees) and your location. The location is not necessarily where you have the hive in the garden, it's broader than that and has more to do with which part of the country you live in. In the UK I have generally found that a bee on the west of the Pennines needs to be a hardy and fairly self-reliant creature, whereas those on the east of the mountains can be a little less hardy. It's all about the climate and how the bees cope with that environment.

Italian bees and British black bees

The most popular bee is the Italian bee or *Apis mellifera ligustica*. It works well in a warm to hot climate, dry conditions and gentle breezes, can cope with high humidity and movement. What it doesn't like is a changeable climate and cold, high winds. This description sums up the weather in much of the UK, and particularly in the north west where I live.

The native British black bee, however, is well suited to the climate in the majority of the UK. The black bee is a good worker and survives well over the winter period. But it is struggling to survive – possibly because of climate change and global warming. Despite the black bee being hardy and durable, something is killing it.

So the majority of bee keepers who breed their own bees have imported species from outside the UK. I have brought in Spanish, Hawaiian and Slovakian queens over the years and their blood line has mixed with the native species.

Scottish bees

I found that the original Scottish black queen that I used was well suited to my home climate, but produced a dirty bee in the way it behaved in the hive. It would leave dead brood in the cells and not clean them out; equally it would allow mess to build up and just work around it. But my Scottish bees settled down well, only needed low numbers to survive through the winter and enjoyed the summer sun that a more southerly environment brought. It was a bee that tended to be feisty, violent or aggressive – depending on how you feel about your experiences with them.

When I introduced a Spanish queen to these Scottish bees I was hoping I could produce a cleaner bee with a less feisty nature. Instead I got a Frankenstein's bee. It was aggressive, violent and downright unpleasant.

Carniolan bees

The year after that we introduced a queen from Hawaii. These bees are known for their pleasant disposition, calm nature and love of hula music, and I brought several to introduce.

They were originally carniolan bees, which appear to have originated from central Europe. It's a strong, hard-working bee that is incredibly popular around the world, and its adaptability is legend.

If you are looking to buy a carniolan queen a good breeder will offer you a selection of three: there are those classed as plains bees, hill bees, and finally mountain bees. If you live somewhere like the vale of York then you are likely to want a plains bee; if you live on the west coast, near Wales or on the moors around Derbyshire or in Devon, you would be better with a hills variety.

Other bees

In the south of England bee keepers will often use an Italian bee because it is well suited to the environment. Occasionally you might find eastern European stock being used – these are generally Caucasian bees. They are slightly grey, and good hard workers that need only small numbers to help them survive over winter. They are a gentle and direct. They know their role in the colony.

If anyone asks you about Africanized bees tell them you don't know and don't want to know. Some people just want to sensationalize the image of bees being killers. Don't get involved: they never have anything constructive to say.

DISEASES AND PESTS

Foul brood

A number of diseases can beset bees, but the two that most bee keepers will come across are AFB (American foul brood) and EFB (European foul brood).

They are similar in nature and spread a disease that is contagious and difficult to remove.

In a case of AFB you have to destroy your hives: frames, wax, honey and bees – everything, in fact. If this happens, don't think that you are a bad or failed bee keeper. You can be as fastidious as possible when it comes to keeping things clean, but contaminated stores and stock, coupled with drifting, can cause the disease to cross colonies. With EFB you can shake the bees off the frame and transfer them to another clean hive, but you will have to destroy the stores and stock.

Varroa mite

Unless you are a bee keeper you may not have heard of AFB and EFB, but many people are aware of the parasitic mite that plagues bees: the varroa destructor mite. The Varroa mite is a circular shaped creature that lives, or rather feasts, on the bees, and by doing so it causes the stock of bees to weaken. They become deformed and other diseases can take hold because the bees are weak. In comparison to the size of the bee, these mites are enormous. Imagine a six-foot man, and then imagine him with three dinner plate-sized mites clutched to his stomach, gently feeding off him – you get the picture.

These mites are resistant to a number of chemicals that have been designed to remove them. Other harsher chemicals appear to upset the bees and even taint the honey. There are a number of 'natural' alternatives, which appear to work well; I use them all the time.

On a dry day in the summer I sometimes dust the bees with icing sugar. Other bees rush to gather the free sugar and in the process knock the mites off the bees they are 'cleaning'. The mite falls to the bottom of the hive, and, there being a mesh floor, it drops out onto the soil, and is unable to get back in.

ENJOY YOUR BEES

Don't get too worried about pests and diseases, though. Like every creature, bees will be affected at some time or other, but there is no need to be concerned most of the time. Enjoy your bees, find your own way with them and the environment. I have advised you to read up on them at first to gain a certain amount of knowledge before you take the plunge, but bee keeping is a craft that you learn over the years. I've kept bees for 35 years and sometimes I feel I haven't even touched the surface.

Get to know your local bee inspector, who can advise you and check your hives for any signs of disease or other problems. Learn on the job, even if that means some heartbreak along the way.

The right choice?

A friend asked me if I regretted giving up my former career to take up bee keeping full time. This is what I told him.

One day in late summer, up on the hills in Lancashire, I was working the bees in the heather. All around me the bees took their flight paths to the bright purple bell and ling heather. The warm air brought the smell of the heather out and the bees worked furiously. I worked with them all day, me and my love affair.

In the early evening I brewed up some tea and ate a cheese and pickle sandwich; I felt as far removed from my previous life in the world of law as humanly possible. I relaxed back into the thick, perfumed heather. Tiny silver planes left vapour trails in the sky. I drifted off listening to the bees buzz and hum above my head.

It was the absence of buzzing and humming that woke me up. Several hours and missed calls later, I awoke from a beautiful sleep, an unconditional sleep that did not urgently drag me back to earth because of work or other commitments. Clearly my change of career had been the right choice.

PART 2
Plants

Introduction

In this part of the book we look at growing three particular types of crops – culinary herbs, soft fruit, and flowers for cutting. These have been chosen over and above other 'grow-ables', in particular vegetables and top, or orchard, fruit. Let me explain first why I haven't dealt with these.

The vegetables that are readily available in greengrocers, supermarkets and market stalls are generally grown on a large-scale, mechanized, commercial basis – this is true even for specialized crops such as Florence fennel – and because of this they can be grown relatively cheaply per 'unit'. A small-scale producer, with a more labour-intensive set-up, simply cannot compete on price, and when it comes to a staple food, such as vegetables, consumers generally look at price first.

So growing vegetables has a small return unless you are producing on a large scale. This is not true of exchanging and bartering, of course, but the chances are that if you have a surplus of one type of vegetable then everyone else in your community will too – and there is a limit to how many jars of green tomato chutney your neighbour might want to make!

Top, or orchard, fruit is not included because if your aim is to make some money as soon as is reasonably possible, then waiting for apple, plum or pear trees to bear fruit – in more ways than one – will be an exercise in thumb-twiddling! However, if you are lucky enough to have an established orchard there may well be an opportunity to cash in on the harvest, although what I have said about vegetables also applies to some degree to apples, plums and pears, unless you have some heritage varieties that would attract a particular group of buyers on a local level. That is not to say that you wouldn't be able to swap or exchange them, but on too many occasions I have been offered bruised windfall apples or over-ripe, squidgy plums in exchange for some honey, an offer that I now politely but firmly decline.

So why are herbs, soft fruit and flowers likely to be good bets? First, they are quite high up in the 'barter' charts; not everyone 'grows their own', and a bunch of garden flowers, for example, appears to be a real bargain to a prolific jam maker when set against a jar of their finest gooseberry and elderflower preserve. Second, herbs, soft fruit and flowers are the sort of crops with which you can 'start small' and then, if time and space allow, you can expand. Third, as long as you have some land – the ultimate 'raw material' – the initial outlay is relatively small. And finally, they are very 'saleable' items, particularly locally at farmers' markets and the like.

The major drawback with all of them is that once harvested they are perishable and have a short 'shelf-life'. The way round this with herbs and fruit can be to use them as an ingredient in something else, rather than them being the 'end product': fruit in jams, for example, or herbs in cheeses and soaps, or growing them in pots. Have a look at the diagram in the Introduction to see how they can be fed into other products that are featured in the book.

It's slightly different with flowers, of course, but even if you don't cut all of them to sell they still present a beautiful display in your garden, and provide food for bees and other beneficial insects – reason enough to grow them.

So if you have green fingers already, or fancy finding out if you have sap or blood in your veins, have a go at growing herbs, fruit, or flowers; the worst that can happen is that they don't – grow, that is.

CHAPTER 4

GROWING HERBS

There is much pleasure to be had from growing herbs in your garden – they are decorative; many, if not all, are aromatic; they attract beneficial insects; and they are relatively easy to grow. As if these were not reasons enough to cultivate them, herbs have a variety of practical uses too – indeed, if herbs were people, then in today's parlance they would be 'multi-taskers'!

Growing herbs can be addictive. A friend of mine has a magnificent herb garden, laid out with lavender hedges and a topiaried bay tree as a centre-piece. She grows a huge range, from everyday parsley to highly poisonous *Aconitum* and her knowledge of herbs is extensive. Her love of herbs started and was nurtured during childhood visits to her grandma once a week. Each time, grandma had prepared something containing different herbs: savoury scones with rosemary, lemon curd tarts with verbena, or there was a piece of hand-dyed material for her to make her doll a new dress. She became curious about all these herbs grandma grew, and so began her 'apprenticeship', as she now calls it. She discovered which herbs were good to eat; that you can use tansy to make a dye; that lavender can help you relax. She learned how to grow them, starting with a few chive seeds in a pot, to taking dozens of cuttings for the lavender hedge.

Despite her enthusiasm and knowledge my friend grows herbs for her own enjoyment and well-being and has never been tempted to turn her pleasure into profit. It is true that nurturing your plants and watching a garden develop brings a sense of satisfaction and contentment and this is justification enough to grow herbs. But you could also build on your interest and look into how you might be able to persuade others to share in your enthusiasm or even make some money.

WHAT SORT OF HERBS SHALL I GROW?

If you are thinking about growing herbs to exchange or sell, by far the best ones to grow for these purposes are culinary ones. Nearly everyone these days uses herbs in their cooking: we have all come across sage and onion stuffing, mint sauce, parsley (even if it is just as a garnish), and pesto, the main ingredient of which is basil, so we are no strangers to their aromatic and flavoursome properties. (Herbs are used for other purposes, of course, like medicine, but this is a science in itself, and unless you have specialist knowledge of these herbs, I would steer clear.)

You could also grow herbs to use in other products, or as a 'raw material' in another process, to 'add value' to another product. For example, you could use herbs in your own home-made preserves, cheese and soaps, or for your own dyeing projects. All these examples are covered later in the book, so we look in this chapter at a number of herbs you can grow to use in some of these products.

WHERE SHALL I GROW MY HERBS?

In beds

If you grow herbs for cutting, particularly if you use a lot of them yourself, they are best grown in a herb bed where they can get their roots down and make strong, abundant growth. If you grow them like this to exchange or sell then you must be certain of a ready market otherwise you may find that your hard work may be going to seed – literally.

You need to make sure that the soil conditions and situation are suitable for the herbs you are growing. The majority of herbs like free-draining soil and a sunny position, but there are exceptions: have a look at the individual entries for herbs later in the chapter.

In pots

Alternatively you could grow them in pots, which is what our expert, Jekka McVicar, does. This makes better sense if you want to exchange them or sell them, because their 'use by date', as it were, would be certainly weeks, if not months, away. As well as having a long 'shelf-life', the other main advantage of growing your herbs in pots is that you can tailor the compost that you use to suit each herb.

POTTING COMPOST

The most straightforward choice is a soil-based compost – but with one or perhaps two 'additives' of your own. Something like a John Innes potting compost, rather than a peat-based one, is the best option. Very few herbs grow in peat and it would be futile to try to grow them in something that would be detrimental to them.

'ADDITIVES'

The first 'additive' is a slow-release fertilizer. This adds to the nutrients already in the compost and will provide sufficient food for the plant until such time as it is sold and its new owner takes over looking after it.

The second 'additive' depends on the herb. For herbs that require a very free-draining soil, such as those that originally hail from Mediterranean regions – rosemary, for example – it is useful to incorporate some perlite, at a rate of three parts compost to one part perlite. Perlite is a generic term for a naturally occurring siliceous rock which has been heat treated to produce light, sterile granules. It has a neutral pH which means that it will not affect the acid or alkaline balance of the soil.

Disadvantages of growing in pots

The main disadvantage is that the plants are unable to search down into the soil for sufficient moisture, so you must provide the water they need. In addition, the extra costs of growing herbs in pots can mount up: compost, the pots themselves, labour costs and so on.

You could also argue that potted herbs are readily available in supermarkets, although whenever I have bought these I have never been able to keep them beyond a few days: it's probably due to the cosseted environment in which they were grown. By growing your herbs 'hard' – namely outside, or under cover with no heating – they will have a much longer lifespan. This also means, however, that your project will be to a degree a seasonal one, restricting the herbs that you can sell all year round to hardy perennial ones, leaving the annuals available during the summer months only.

Choices to make when growing in pots

If you sell herbs in pots, you need to decide what sort of pots you are going to use; how you will label them; and how much you will charge.

TYPE OF POT

A variety of pots are available in different sizes and made from different materials. From a quick survey of my local garden centres and nurseries it appears that the majority of herbs come in plastic, 9cm round pots, while some larger plants are sold in 1 litre, and larger, plastic pots. As for the most part garden centres and nurseries act as 'middle men', buying in plants from wholesale growers and selling them on with little or no intervention, we can assume that the wholesale growers deem this shape and size of pot to be the most economical. So if you choose this option, you must be prepared to compete with garden centres and nurseries on price.

The alternative is to go for something different, in terms of either size, shape, or material, so that your pots stand out from the crowd: for example, using a square pot of a different colour, or embracing a more environmentally friendly approach by using biodegradable pots.

LABELS

What sort of label will you use – 'stick in' or 'stick on', professionally produced or 'home-made'? How much information are you going to give – just the name of the plant, or with further growing instructions? And what about some recipes or suggestions for using your herb in the kitchen? More decisions!

PRICING

Before you can price your herbs you should calculate your costings – how much has it actually cost you to get them to the point where they can be sold – and also decide what profit margin is reasonable. Only then will you have an approximate selling figure. You need to be aware of what other retailers are charging for a *similar* product. If a local garden centre is offering pots of herbs for, say, £1.50, it is not sensible to charge £2 for yours – unless, of course, yours are special in some way in which case you may be justified in charging a premium.

DECIDING WHAT CULINARY HERBS TO GROW

Ultimately the choice is yours. Some herbs are extremely popular and perhaps these should form the basis of your collection (marked 'B' below), like parsley, sage, rosemary and thyme – I feel a song coming on! In addition there are some that are not so widely used but are still worth growing – the 'special collection' (marked 'S' below), like summer savory and sweet cicely.

Herbs to grow from seed

BASIL

Basil (B) (*Ocimum basilicum*) is a tender annual so must be grown from seed. Unless you have a heated propagator there is no point in sowing it too early because it needs a minimum night temperature of $13°C$ to ensure germination. No fewer than 17 different varieties are listed in one herb catalogue, but the most popular is sweet or Genovese basil, which is the one used in pesto sauce. You could experiment with growing others, but beware that you aren't left with them at the end of the season.

One tip that I have found extremely useful is to always water the plant from below, and never after midday. This helps to prevent damping off, to which basil plants are particularly prone for some reason.

CELERY LEAF

Celery leaf (S) (*Apium graveolens*) is a biennial grown as an annual. Unlike 'normal' celery (*A. graveolens* var. *dulce*), which is grown for its crunchy stems, celery leaf is grown for its – leaves! Celery leaf has been developed from smallage, a herb grown widely in former times for its celery flavour but with the disadvantage that it is poisonous when raw and extremely bitter. Celery leaf has had this toxicity and bitterness bred out of it, although some people still find it a little too astringent for their palate. Celery leaf is also known as par-cel because it looks like parsley but tastes like celery.

CHERVIL

Chervil (S) (*Anthriscus cerefolium*) is a biennial, but like parsley is best grown as an annual. It is not a sun-worshipper and will rapidly run to seed if the conditions are too hot or dry. Chervil is widely used in French cookery, being one of the ingredients of *fines herbes*, but is not frequently found in English dishes – so now is your chance to spread the word!

CHIVES AND GARLIC CHIVES

Chives (B) (*Allium schoenoprasum*) and garlic chives (S) (*A. tuberosum*) are members of the onion family. While 'ordinary' chives have a mild, oniony flavour, the garlic variety has a mild, sweet, garlic flavour. They both like rich, moist soil which must not be allowed to dry out during the growing season, so don't put any perlite in the compost. If you don't sell all your plants in the first season, they are easily divided in the autumn to make two or three new specimens from each pot.

CORIANDER

Coriander (B) (*Coriandrum sativum*) is best grown in light shade because a combination of sun and too little water will quickly result in it running to seed. For a good supply of plants, sow a succession of seed throughout the summer.

DILL

Dill (B) (*Anethum graveolens*) has feathery leaves resembling fennel but its flavour is quite different: dill has a mild, warm flavour, while fennel has an aniseed taste. Dill is widely used in Scandinavia and northern, central and eastern Europe, but is not often found in Mediterranean dishes. It has a wonderful affinity with almost all fish dishes, especially salmon, and goes well with summer vegetables such as beans, courgettes, tender young spinach leaves and cucumber.

LOVAGE

Lovage (S) (*Levisticum officinale*) used to be widely grown but seems to have fallen out of favour. It has quite a strong flavour and its leaves and crushed seeds can be used sparingly as a salt substitute. It likes moisture-retentive soil, and will quickly outgrow a small pot so don't propagate too many unless you are sure of your market.

OREGANO

Oregano (B) (*Origanum vulgare*) is one of the hardiest members of the *Origanum* family, which makes it the best one to grow for our purposes. It needs well-drained soil, so it is worth adding some perlite to your compost. It grows easily from seed, but you can also take cuttings from established plants to increase your stock.

PARSLEY

Parsley (B) (*Petroselinum crispum*) is a biennial that is best grown as an annual because in its second year it will run to seed very quickly. The most common types are the curly leaved parsley (*P. crispum*) and the flat leaved, French or Italian parsley (S) (*P. crispum* var. *Neapolitanum*).

SUMMER SAVORY

Summer savory (S) (*Satureja hortensis*) is a real sun-worshipper and requires well-drained soil, so add some extra perlite to your compost. The leaves add a lovely peppery or spicy flavour to many dishes. In continental Europe and America it is commonly called the 'bean herb' because it has a particular affinity with all bean dishes.

SWEET CICELY

Sweet cicely (S) (*Myrrhis odorata*) is one of the more unusual herbs to grow, but it is worthwhile because its leaves, which have a sweet, slightly aniseed flavour, have long been used as a sugar substitute, particularly in fruit dishes. It likes a moisture-retentive soil. A word of warning: its appearance can easily be confused with cow parsley (*Anthriscus sylvestris*) which is not poisonous, or the deadly hemlock (*Conium maculatum*) which it also resembles. Be sure to reassure your customers that you are in fact selling sweet cicely!

Herbs to grow from cuttings

BAY

Bay (B) (*Laurus nobilis*) is really the one evergreen shrub that no herb garden should be without. You can propagate bay by taking cuttings, but you will have to wait several years before they are of sufficient size to sell. I have found that buying in small, established plants is the best way forward. You can also offer larger, clipped shrubs which make splendid focal points in the herb garden.

HYSSOP

Hyssop (S) (*Hyssopus officinalis*) used to be widely grown but is often overlooked nowadays. Its leaves have a warm, spicy flavour, suggestive of a mixture of thyme, rosemary and mint – ideal for any number of recipes. It demands free-draining soil, so add some perlite to the compost.

LEMON VERBENA

Lemon verbena (S) (*Aloysia triphylla*) is one of those herbs that once anyone smells it they will want to grow it: when you crush its leaves you are instantly reminded of lemon sherbet sweets! It is half-hardy and will struggle with temperatures below 4°C so you must protect your plants over winter. Again, free-draining soil is called for.

MINT

Mentha spicata (B) is the most common garden mint, and, to my mind, still the best despite the availability of numerous other varieties. Most people want mint for their mint sauce and this is the one to use. It needs fairly moist soil, so don't add any perlite to your compost. It can be very invasive if left to its own devices in the herb garden – something to point out to customers.

ROSEMARY

Rosemary (B) (*Rosmarinus officinalis*) hails from the Mediterranean region. It likes lots of sun and free-draining soil, so you need to make sure you add some perlite to your compost. It is evergreen, which makes it a good herb to sell all year round.

SAGE

Salvia officinalis (B) is the common, garden or broad-leaved sage and is the best-known sage for culinary use. It has pale grey-green, velvety leaves. Other varieties have colourful leaves, notably gold sage (S) (*S. officinalis* 'Icterina') or purple sage (S) (*S. officinalis* Purpurascens group), and are just as good in the kitchen, although their flavour might not be as strongly aromatic as the common sage. It needs free-draining soil.

TARRAGON

Tarragon (B) (*Artemisia dracunculus*) comes in two varieties – French (*A. dracunculus*) and Russian (*A. dracunculus dracunculoides*). By far the best is the French because of its superior flavour. It does not produce viable seed so must be propagated by cuttings. It is also a little on the tender side and requires some protection during the winter. It needs free-draining soil.

THYME

According to the Royal Horticultural Society (www.rhs.org.uk) there are about 350 species of thyme (including three that grow wild in Britain). Garden or common thyme (B) (*Thymus vulgaris*), lemon thyme (S) (*Thymus* x *citriodorus*) and broad-leaved thyme (S) (*T. pulegioides*) are the three most widely used in the kitchen. All need free-draining soil.

WINTER SAVORY

Winter savory (S) (*Satureja montana*) is the perennial version of summer savory. It has a slightly more robust flavour than its annual cousin but requires the same growing conditions. It is semi-evergreen so will hold some of its leaves over winter.

GROWING HERBS FOR 'ADDED VALUE'

Herbs can also be grown for use as a raw material in another product. Later in the book there are chapters on making sweet preserves (Chapter 8), cheese (Chapter 7), and soaps (Chapter 11), and also one on dyeing (Chapter 12). Herbs could be used in any one of these so here are a few that might be suited to each of these projects.

Herbs for sweet preserves

The number of herbs that you can add to sweet preserves – things like jam, marmalade and curds – is quite limited, but I am concentrating on these because sweet preserves making is covered later in the book. (If you are making savoury preserves, such as chutneys and relishes, then the range of herbs that you can use is far greater.)

Some 'sweet' herbs that you can use include sweet cicely and lemon verbena (see above), angelica and lavender.

ANGELICA

Angelica (*Angelica archangelica*) is a hardy, biennial, monocarpic plant, which means that it dies after setting seed. In fact, it is best grown from seed sown in situ because mature plants do not transplant well. It likes deep, moist soil.

LAVENDER

Although you can use the leaves of lavender (*Lavandula* sp.), it is the flowers – either fresh or dried – that are of most use in preserve making. Lavender needs well-drained soil and a sunny position.

Herbs for cheese

Although the most common herbs to use in cheese making are chives, parsley and rosemary, you could, theoretically, use any of the culinary herbs to add flavour to your cheese or to coat it.

It would perhaps be worth experimenting a little to find a 'signature' blend from the herbs looked at in the previous section – cheese experts Martin and Gill Russell use lavender flowers in their very special brie, for example.

Herbs for soaps

Some herbs work better in handmade soaps than others but tried and tested ones seem to be lavender flowers, rosemary, lemon verbena, thyme (all detailed above) and pot marigold. Our soap expert, Linda Clough (see Chapter 11), makes a gardener's soap which contains finely chopped parsley – not only is it a lovely colour, it also has slightly deodorizing properties.

POT MARIGOLD
Pot marigold (*Calendula officinalis*) is a hardy annual with large orange or yellow daisy-like flowers. The flowers, either fresh or dried, can be used in soaps and dyes. It will grow in almost any soil, the exception being waterlogged conditions.

Herbs for dyeing

Colour can be extracted from almost any plant – but some will result in more pleasing colours than others. In fact until the relatively recent introduction of chemical-based dyes, plants provided the only source of dye. Some people still prefer the 'natural' colour that can be obtained from plant-based dyes, and it can be worth growing some of your own dye plants, although often quite a large number of flowers or leaves are required to produce an adequate amount of dye, so bear this in mind when you are planning your 'dyer's garden'. Teresinha Roberts, our dye expert (see Chapter 12), started off by growing three basic dye herbs – woad, madder and weld – in a spare corner of her allotment and now she has a thriving business. Have a look at Chapter 12 for some suggestions for other herbs to grow.

CASE STUDY – JEKKA MCVICAR

Jekka McVicar has progressed from growing herbs in her back garden to become an internationally renowned herb grower. Here is her story, in her own words.

'As a child, unlike many of my friends who wanted to work with horses, I wanted to be a bio-physicist. I never, ever thought I would become a herb farmer. I grew up in a village in the West Country, a child of the fifties, where my mother was totally self-sufficient and my grandmother wrote amazing cookbooks. My father's side of the family were all intense gardeners and pontificated in Latin about their plants so much that I was, as a child, definitely not interested in plants or gardens. But for as long as I can remember, I was in love with good food and the growing of food, which I did not, for some reason, class as plants.

'My career before growing herbs professionally was very varied: I was a flautist in a rock band playing at the Isle of Wight with Bob Dylan, playing at the first Glastonbury; this was followed by a period of working for the BBC, followed by community TV; then starting the second police video unit in the UK for Avon and Somerset Constabulary. During this period I was always cooking, always using fresh herbs and when I had my first garden, also growing vegetables.

'The herb farm started in the early 1980s in the back garden of our semi-detached house in Filton, Bristol. A girl friend of mine happened to ask if she could pick some French tarragon from my garden as she was cooking an Elizabeth David recipe. I realized that there was a demand for fresh herbs, as they were not available in supermarkets or shops and only a few in garden centres.

'Within a matter of months of starting I had three greengrocer shops, one garden centre and two health food stores all wanting plants. I used all the space in the house to grow them and we made cold frames for outside. From the very start I chose to be organic, as I did not see the necessity of using chemicals and I did not want my children to be excluded from the business in any way, and if I had used chemicals they would have been.

'The orders built up so fast that space became a serious problem. Then one day my husband gave me an ultimatum: 'Either give it up now or let's move and make this into a proper business.' So in 1987 we moved. We found a derelict cottage with an acre of land, and lived in a mobile home while we did it up.

'But the driving force was herb growing, so we're still, over 25 years later, doing up our cottage. Back then we grew only 35 varieties of herb. Today we grow over 650 varieties, and supply celebrity chefs as well as mail order herbs. We are certified organic by the Soil Association, and have been awarded over 60 RHS gold medals including 14 at the Chelsea Flower Show. Over the years I've written five books about herbs, growing and their uses, the latest of which, *Jekka's Herb Cookbook*, was illustrated by my daughter Hannah.

'Horticulture is hard work, and my business wouldn't have thrived without the endless support of my family. But it's my life-blood and my passion; my favourite place in the world is my glasshouse where I can see and feel the plants growing. I cannot think of a more amazing group of plants to grow and preserve for future generations, for they look good, smell good and do you good – what more can you ask from a group of plants?'

CHAPTER 5

GROWING SOFT FRUIT

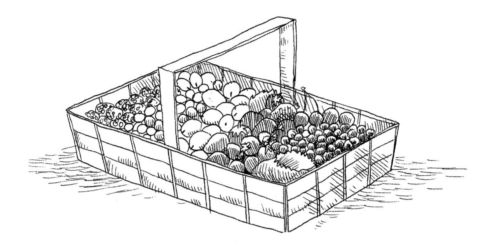

Eating freshly picked, home-grown fruit has to be one of the most satisfying, and flavoursome, experiences I have ever had. As a child I remember helping my mum harvest the first strawberries of the season and being allowed to pop one into my mouth, still warm from the sun – the taste is an abiding memory. I am often disappointed these days to find that the flavour and succulence of bought ones isn't as I remember it: is it the strawberries, or am I just getting old? Certainly, once the fruit is picked it starts to deteriorate, no matter how quickly it gets from plot to plate, so sometimes fruit can be several days old before you get to eat it, losing a good deal of its flavour on the way. And I am undeniably older!

To try and 'recapture' some of the strawberries of my childhood I grow a couple of rows in my garden. The harvest is modest rather than abundant, but it is enough. If I had the room I might be tempted to plant more types of fruit and in larger quantities, not only for myself but to sell as well. This is what

Rose Shepherd, our soft fruit expert, did some years ago, when 'pick your own' was in its heyday – more about Rose later.

You might be wondering which fruits to grow. Unless you already have an established orchard of apples, pears or plums it is probably not worth thinking about planting this type of fruit with a view to generating some extra income – it will take too long for them to produce a worthwhile crop. You can, of course, plant up an orchard for your own enjoyment – and if you keep hens (see Chapter 1), they will love roaming around it too.

If you want to make a little money from your fruit growing endeavours, though, soft fruit will produce a crop either in the very same year they are planted, or soon after.

REGIONAL GROWING

Historically there are regions in the UK that are associated with growing particular types of fruit, and you may want to revive or continue this practice in your own area. For example, Cambridgeshire is traditionally linked with growing strawberries, which is apparent from the name of some of the varieties, such as 'Cambridge Favourite' and 'Early Cambridge'. Lancashire and Cheshire are renowned for their gooseberries, central Scotland for its raspberries. As long as you have suitable soil and a sunny aspect, however, you can grow whatever you like and whatever you think will sell locally.

WHERE SHOULD I GROW MY FRUIT?

Getting the soil right

To grow soft fruit you should ideally have fertile, well-drained but moisture-retentive soil which is friable to a depth of at least 30cm for strawberries and 45cm for cane fruit, such as raspberries, and bush fruit, such as currants. If your soil is nothing like this you will have to prepare it by digging it thoroughly and incorporating some well-rotted organic matter, and some horticultural grit if necessary.

It should also be slightly acid with a pH of about 6.5. You can test the pH of your soil with a soil-testing kit, available from garden centres. If your soil is too acid (below 5.8) you will have to add some garden lime at the rate indicated on the packet. If it is too alkaline you can remedy this by applying iron and manganese, available in proprietary form from garden centres.

Getting the right aspect

A sunny area is the place to grow fruit. Most fruits will tolerate some shade, but you may not get such a good yield. Fruit also likes a sheltered position where it will not be buffeted by strong winds. If necessary erect a windbreak to protect your precious fruits.

DECIDING WHAT FRUIT TO GROW

This will really depend on how much room you have — and, arguably more importantly, what you enjoy growing. If you can't stand the sight of gooseberries there is not much point growing them just because you think they may be a lucrative crop. It's better to grow something that inspires you and will encourage you to look after them: you will reap the rewards — literally!

Strawberries

Strawberries are extremely popular, they are a fairly efficient crop to grow and they attract a comparatively high price, all of which makes them top of my 'best fruit to grow' list.

You can plant strawberries in open ground, which is the traditional way of growing them. They need good, fertile soil which has had a good amount of well-rotted manure dug into it: the plants will fruit successfully for up to four years, so they need a well-prepared bed to start with. Plant the crowns, as the strawberry plants are known, 45cm apart in rows that are 60cm apart in August or September to crop the following year.

As the fruits develop they are bedded on a layer of straw to protect them from being splashed by soil if it rains, and also to help deter slugs making a meal of them. Special strawberry 'mats' which surround the plant and do the same job are available. Or you could plant them through a permeable membrane which has the added bonus of keeping down some of the weeds that will inevitably set seed in your lovely fertile soil.

The main purpose of this protection, in whatever form it takes, is to keep the berries as clean and blemish-free as possible: dirty or damaged fruit are much less desirable in the eyes of the consumer. This is also why it is a good idea to protect the fruit from birds. I don't mind birds having a few of my fruits but I have witnessed a blackbird go along a row pecking at every berry without eating one whole fruit. I net my rows and despite my fears that birds may become entangled in it, so far this hasn't happened.

You must make sure that your plants have sufficient water, especially in dry spells, otherwise the fruits will not develop properly. Be careful to keep water away from ripening berries, though, because it could encourage grey mould.

'TABLETOP' GROWING
There is another method of growing strawberries that cuts out bending down, weeding, and having to bed the fruits on straw – and there are no soil-borne diseases or slugs. You grow your plants in growing bags that have been raised off the ground: this system has been adopted by many commercial growers.

The major drawbacks with this method are, first, that because the roots are restricted inside the growing bags the plants are entirely dependent on you to provide the water they need, and second, that the nutrients in the growing medium will soon be used and you have to provide extra food in the form of slow-release fertilizer. Weighing up the pros and cons, I may soon be adopting this system of growing, if only for the sake of my back.

VARIETIES
There are three categories of strawberries: summer-fruiting, perpetual or remontant, and alpine.

Growing at least three different varieties of summer-fruiting berries means that you can have ripe fruit from early to late summer. Early summer varieties include 'Christine' and 'Honeoye'; mid summer ones include 'Cambridge Favourite' and 'Royal Sovereign'; late summer varieties include 'Florence' and 'Symphony'.

Perpetual or remontant varieties crop intermittently throughout the summer until the first frosts. Try 'Malling Opal' or, my favourite, 'Mara des Bois'.

Alpine strawberries are usually grown from seed and are replaced after two years. The fruits are much smaller than 'ordinary' strawberries but what they lack in size they make up for in flavour. Good varieties include 'Alexandria' and 'Fraise des Bois'. And if you can bear to set some of these berries aside for jam, replace a handful or two of 'ordinary' strawberries with alpine ones in your favourite recipe – the result will be beyond words.

Cane fruit
Blackberries and raspberries (and other hybrid berries like loganberries and tayberries) produce fruit on canes which need support. Stout posts with three rows of wires tensioned between them are just the job.

BLACKBERRIES

When it comes to growing blackberries my advice is to grow a thornless variety – otherwise you might as well scour the hedgerows for wild blackberries (or brambles as they are commonly known) and have your arms shredded that way. Blackberry thorns are vicious and will reduce greatly the pleasure you gain from growing and picking these luscious fruits. Make life easier for yourself and choose varieties like 'Loch Tay', 'Loch Ness' or 'Oregon Thornless'. You will get bigger fruits and higher yields than from the native blackberry – between 4.5kg and 12kg per plant, depending on the variety.

Blackberries are vigorous plants so take this into account when deciding how many plants to grow. Some varieties need to be spaced up to 4 metres apart.

The fruit is borne on year-old canes, so once a cane has produced berries it should be untied from its support and cut down to ground level. New canes which grow from the base can now be tied in to replace the old ones.

RASPBERRIES

Raspberries are my favourite fruit: there seems to be just the right amount of sweetness very slightly tinged with tanginess that gets my taste buds popping. And what would a scone be without home-made raspberry jam?

There are basically two kinds of raspberries – summer-fruiting and autumn-fruiting. Summer-fruiting varieties, such as 'Malling Minerva' and 'Tulameen', produce berries on the previous year's growth. They should be pruned as you would blackberries: as soon as fruiting has finished cut the old canes down to ground level. Between four and eight new young canes can then be selected to replace the old ones. If the plant, or stool, has produced in excess of eight, cut these out so that as much vigour as possible is directed into your chosen ones.

Autumn-fruiting canes, such as 'Autumn Bliss' and 'Polka', bear fruit on the current season's growth. All the canes should be cut to ground level each

February, and the stool will produce new canes in the spring and these will bear fruit in the autumn of the same year.

On average you can expect to pick almost 700g of berries from each plant over the season. This will depend on the number of fruiting canes there are per stool and the weather, but if you have a 5-metre row you can expect to harvest about 7.5kg: raspberry stools should be planted about 45cm apart.

Bush fruit

BLUEBERRIES

Blueberries go by a number of names: they are also known as bilberries or whortleberries. Blueberries are a very expensive fruit to buy in the shops, which probably makes them a sound bet if you wish to make a little income from your fruit venture.

Blueberries are members of the *Ericaceae* family and this gives a clue to the sort of growing conditions they like. They require a moist but well-drained, humus-rich, and above all, acid soil. The acidity is of vital importance: a pH of 4.0–5.5 is called for, which would be way too acid for many plants. If your soil is not acid enough it is usually enough just to dig out a 45cm square hole and fill this with ericaceous compost before planting your blueberry bush. If you then mulch regularly with ericaceous compost this should be sufficient for your plants to thrive: if not, give them a dose of ericaceous fertilizer (the sort garden centres sell to give your rhododendrons or azaleas a boost) at the recommended rate on the packet and they should be happy.

The most widely grown variety is 'Bluecrop' but there are others such as 'Chandler' and 'Duke'. Yield varies but I have heard of some mature plants producing up to 9kg. You should plant your bushes 1.2 to 1.5 metres apart. Regular pruning is not essential, but regular watering is.

BLACKCURRANTS

Blackcurrants seem to be universally liked, even if it is only in the form of a well-known fruit squash! You rarely see the fruits on sale in supermarkets or greengrocers but they are delicious, especially if they are jostling together with some strawberries and raspberries in a summer pudding, and, to my mind, should be more widely available. So now is your chance! Harvesting them is a doddle: you simply snip off the bunches of berries and pop them into a punnet – and if you line the punnet with a couple of leaves, they look even more attractive.

Blackcurrant bushes are really stools, rather than one single stem with branches coming from it. The best fruit is carried on stems produced the previous summer, although older wood will still crop. The idea, then, is to have a succession of strong, healthy stems year on year to replace the older stems, which should be cut as near to the base of the plant as possible when you remove them. A healthy plant will last for up to 15 years if well cared for and fed.

You should plant your blackcurrant bushes about 1.5 metres apart and prune them hard initially – cut all the shoots down to about 5cm. This will encourage the production of strong young stems from the base.

Some of the best varieties are in the 'Ben' series, such as 'Ben Connan', 'Ben Hope' and 'Ben Lomond'. You can expect about 4.5kg of fruit per bush in a reasonable season.

RED AND WHITE CURRANTS

Red and white currants belong to the same genus as blackcurrants (*Ribes*) but they grow differently from one another. Red and white currants grow from a permanent 'skeleton' of branches rather than a succession of new stems.

Pruning them is a little more involved than pruning blackcurrants: in the spring of the first year after you have planted them you should remove all except five main stems, cutting them back to the base. The five remaining stems should be pruned back to 15–20cm. Each year after that there are two stages of pruning: in midsummer (mid-June to July) you should cut back the current season's growth to five leaves – unless you want to extend the size of your bush, in which case you can leave some branches alone. Then in winter, prune all the side shoots growing from the 'framework' branches to one to three buds. You should also shorten the tips of the branches by about a quarter, cutting just above an outward-facing bud. (This pruning regime is the same for gooseberries.)

Although we talk of red and white currants as if they are different species, the white currant is really just a mutation, or sport, of the redcurrant. For that reason they are treated the same as far as cultivation is concerned – the only discernible difference is the colour of the fruit.

You should plant your currant bushes about 1.5 metres apart. As far as yield goes, you can expect between 3.5 and 4.5kg of fruit per bush. 'Jonkheer van Tets' and 'Rovada' are two good redcurrant varieties, with 'White Versailles' being the most widely grown white currant.

GOOSEBERRIES

Gooseberries are one of those things in life that you either love or hate. I love them, especially lightly stewed in a little water and honey with some elderflowers thrown in.

Gooseberries have long been a speciality of northern and midland counties. In the 1750s some Lancashire weavers founded gooseberry clubs, with their resulting shows, where they strived to grow and show the biggest, plumpest gooseberry. Interest soon spread to Yorkshire, Cheshire, Derbyshire, Staffordshire and Nottinghamshire and clubs and shows sprang up across the entire region. Shows are still staged today, particularly in Cheshire, although the oldest show, dating back to 1800, takes place in Egton Bridge in Yorkshire each August.

Older varieties are still available, such as 'Lancashire Lad' and 'London', although some have a tendency to be on the tart side as far as flavour goes. Newer varieties, such as 'Hinnonmaki Yellow' and 'Hinnonmaki Red', are often much sweeter. As you can guess by their names, the berries are of different colours which make a very attractive combination if you mix the fruits together.

You can expect to pick about 3kg of fruit from each bush, which should be planted 1.2 to 1.5 metres apart. Pruning is the same as for redcurrants.

RHUBARB

Rhubarb is not strictly a fruit since it is the stalk of the plant that we eat. It is so often lumped together with soft fruit, and it crops earlier than the 'proper' fruit, that it is worth including it here. It used to be eaten more widely, possibly because in days gone by it bridged the gap between the last of the stored apples and the first fruits of summer.

Rhubarb has been grown for many years in the so-called 'Rhubarb Triangle' in Yorkshire, which comprises the area between Bradford, Wakefield and Leeds – and it still is. This is mostly 'forced' rhubarb, grown in darkened sheds with only the minimum of lighting. This rhubarb is tender and has a much more delicate flavour than outdoor-grown rhubarb. You can imitate this practice by putting some rhubarb forcing pots over the crowns, which have already been covered with a layer of straw or bracken, in December or January. You will be able to harvest some stems two to three weeks earlier than you normally would.

When you harvest the stems you must pull them away from the plant rather than cut them – this way there will be no stump left behind to rot.

Whatever varieties you choose, you should not harvest any stems for the first season after planting in order to build up the plant's vigour. Thereafter you should take no more than half the total stems at any one time, and then only those that are about 30cm long, and you should stop harvesting altogether in July or August.

Although rhubarb is often relegated to the scruffiest part of the garden it actually repays some tender loving care with an abundant crop. Its requirements are the same as for any other fruit: well-prepared, fertile soil, preferably in full sun. Give your plants a good mulch of organic matter in the spring and autumn, but don't protect the crowns over winter: they need a period of exposure to the cold to break their dormancy.

My allotment friends tell me that these varieties are the best: 'Early Champagne', 'Stockbridge Arrow' and 'Victoria'. I have always grown 'Timperley Early' but apparently you get better results with 'Stockbridge Arrow', a newer variety, bred in Yorkshire.

One point to remember is that you should not let your rhubarb plant produce flowers. If you see a flower erupting, pull it out otherwise all the plant's energy will be directed into the flowering stem rather than the leafing stems, which are the ones you want to harvest.

THE BIRDS AND THE BEES

Birds

Birds love fruit. Unless you don't mind sharing your hard-earned crop with the local avian population you will have to protect your fruit from their ravaging beaks. Blackbirds can strip a blackcurrant bush in a matter of minutes so it is as well to be prepared.

You can protect your fruit in a couple of ways. The most effective – but most expensive – is to enclose the whole lot in a fruit cage: the economics of such an undertaking would have to be carefully considered. A cheaper option is to drape each plant, or row of plants, with lightweight netting or mesh which can be easily drawn back when you want to harvest some fruit.

Bees

You need an effective means of pollinating the flowers. By far the most efficient pollinator of plants grown for their fruit is the bee. The blossom of all the fruit we have considered is easily accessible by both bumble and honey bees, so if you have been inspired to keep some honey bees after reading Chapter 3 then you will be able to provide some pollen and nectar for them. And it could be that you will have an even bigger crop as a result of our buzzy friends' activity.

A point to note is that if you grow your fruit inside a cage you must remember to open it during the flowering period because insects, and especially bees, will not readily enter an enclosed space. This will not be a problem if you are just draping your bushes; you would only be doing this when the fruit begins to ripen.

DEALING WITH THE FRUIT YOU HARVEST

There are three principal ways of dealing with the fruit you harvest, apart from eating it all yourself straight away! You can sell it, soon after you have picked it, you can 'add value' to it by using it as an ingredient in something else, like sweet preserves, or you can freeze what you can't eat to use later. If we are assuming that you want to grow some fruit to generate a little income we can disregard the last option, which leaves us with selling it fresh or using it in something else. Let's look at these in reverse order.

Using your excess fruit

I have said 'excess' because you will be certain to eat some of the fruit yourself – but we are hoping that you will have some left over, even after your most voracious indulgence.

Perhaps the most obvious way you could use your excess fruit is to make it into jam: this is certainly one of the most popular ways because the resulting product will keep for a long time, and once you have tasted home-made jam you will not be interested in shop-bought again. Have a look at the chapter on sweet preserves (Chapter 8) if you are inspired to make some yourself. And, of course, jam is something you can sell.

You could use your fruit in baked products: I am thinking particularly of pies and tarts, which you could make for yourself or to sell. My family's favourite is a mixed fruit pie, made with blackberries, raspberries and blackcurrants, sweetened with honey, and served with a dollop of clotted cream.

An enterprising friend of mine makes mead (from honey collected from his own bees) and added some fruit to his 'brew' as an experiment. The resulting concoction is very tasty indeed, especially the one with blackberries.

When you are picking fruit you can't help ending up with stained fingers, which gives you a clue to another way of using your excess fruit – as a dyestuff. Blackberry fruits give lovely shades of purple/lavender, as do blackcurrants. If you use redcurrants you will end up with red/brown shades, rather than a vibrant vermilion. And don't throw away the leaves of your rhubarb when you pull the stems – they can be used to make a pale yellow/green colour, and the roots produce a much deeper, brighter yellow.

It is worth experimenting with other fruits to see what you end up with, although I can't see any of my precious strawberries or raspberries ending up this way: summer pudding pot, yes – dye pot, no!

Selling your fruit

Like much other home-grown produce you will rarely have enough to supply a retail outlet such as a greengrocer on a regular basis. You could sell it direct, either at your gate or through a market outlet, like a farmers' market or country market (have a look at Chapter 14). Alternatively you could offer it direct to someone locally who makes preserves, or some other product that makes use of your fruit.

Whatever you decide to do with your surplus fruit you can be sure that there will be a ready market and you will wish you had even more!

CASE STUDY – ROSE SHEPHERD

Rose Shepherd has retired now and no longer grows fruit, but she is an oracle when it comes to strawberries and raspberries. Rose had a smallholding in Bedfordshire, the majority of which she rented out as pasture for ponies, but she kept a portion of it for herself. She grew her own vegetables and fruit on it, nurtured and sustained by copious amounts of stable manure which her 'pony girls', as she called them, were only too pleased to get rid of.

She was growing organically without realizing that she was – she eschewed artificial fertilizers and pesticides, relying on what nature provided in terms of manure and beneficial bugs. She did struggle with the weather sometimes, though. The rainfall in Bedfordshire is scant to say the least so despite her strict regime of mulching she had to irrigate her crops occasionally. Rain at the wrong time also caused problems – one year her entire crop of strawberries was destroyed because of a prolonged wet spell. And slugs often had a field day, so not everything in the garden was always rosy.

When she decided to increase the amount of fruit she was growing she stuck to her 'organic' beliefs. Although the harvest may not have been as bountiful, the flavour of the fruit was second to none, which is why, she believes, she always managed to sell any excess she had, sometimes within hours of it being put on her improvised sales counter (an old wooden wheelbarrow with a garden umbrella attached) at the gate.

The amount of work gradually increased in line with the amount of land given over to strawberries and raspberries, until it got to the point where fruit was being left on the plants because Rose simply didn't have enough hours in a day to pick it. She freely admits she hadn't thought the whole enterprise through properly: 'It just took over, really,' she says. 'I enjoyed the actual growing bit and didn't think enough about what would happen when all the fruit started ripening.'

It was then that she decided to join the PYO ('pick your own') brigade, where the public would, literally, come and pick their own fruit, and pay for it by weight. 'Some people cheated,' Rose chuckles. 'While they were picking, they would eat as much as they put in the basket. But too much of a good thing gives you stomach ache – especially strawberries! I never minded, because they only did it once.'

She also continued with 'gate' sales and says that if farmers' markets had been around at the zenith of her growing career she would have been the first to book a place – she thinks they are a brilliant way of connecting the consumer with the producer, something that she has always been keen to promote.

Would she go down the PYO route now? 'No. There's too much to worry about with the public coming on your land. We didn't have so much health and safety stuff back then,' she explains. Would she still grow fruit, though? 'No doubt,' she says. 'I remember the taste of the first raspberry of the season – that alone made it all worthwhile.'

CHAPTER 6

GROWING FLOWERS FOR CUTTING

Flowers have an unerring ability to bring a smile to people's faces. There is nothing quite like a bunch of flowers to lift your spirits, brighten a dull day, convey how much you care for someone, to say thank you, mark a special occasion – the list is endless.

The most memorable bunch I have ever been given was a modest bunch of garden flowers. In monetary terms it was not worth an awful lot, but to me it was priceless because the person giving it to me had grown the flowers themselves. And it sparked off an idea.

Every week or so I used to buy flowers from the florist or supermarket that were for the most part imported, or grown in heated greenhouses, or both. And yet here was a bunch of equally lovely home-grown flowers. I decided there and then to turn part of my garden over to growing my own flowers for cutting. There would be no 'flower miles' to worry my conscience, and I could grow the blooms I like. The main disadvantage that I could see was that there would be few, if any, blooms to gather during the winter months. But there would be greenery. And I would appreciate the flowers even more when they did appear.

My cutting garden – patch, really – is very modest but I grow enough during the season for myself and to give away occasionally to friends. And I encourage all my gardening friends to do the same; one is toying with the idea of extending her cutting plot so that she can grow additional flowers to sell at our local farmers' market.

WHAT DO I NEED TO GET STARTED?

Before you start there are three things you need: a love of flowers, decent soil and the correct location.

Passion

There can be nothing more soul-destroying than having to bend your back day after day growing something you have no enthusiasm for. Make no mistake; growing things is hard labour as well as a labour of love. If you grow flowers without an underlying passion for them they will become little more than another commodity. So think carefully – do you love them enough?

Preparing the soil

A much more matter-of-fact requirement is good soil: it needs to be neutral, fertile and well drained but moisture retentive. If your soil isn't like that already you must spend time and effort making it so, otherwise all your subsequent labour will be in vain.

A good variety of flowers will grow on alkaline or acid soil, but the number that will grow well in these conditions is limited. Far better if you have a neutral soil, which is the type preferred by the vast majority of flowers. You may need to dig in copious amounts of organic matter in the form of well-rotted manure or compost: this will increase the fertility and aid with drainage and moisture retention. Incorporate some grit if your soil is not as well drained as you would like. I can't emphasize enough how important it is to get the soil right first.

Choice of location

Just as most of the flowers you will be growing prefer a neutral soil, the majority prefer a sunny open site, but sheltered from the wind. If the area you are earmarking for your flowers is in constant shade, or on an exposed hillside, think again – they will no doubt survive, but they will not thrive and your harvest will be poor.

DECIDING HOW MANY FLOWERS TO GROW

This depends on how much space you have available. To give you a rough idea, if your aim is to cut six or eight bunches a week in the high season and two bunches a week before and after that you will need about 12 square metres in total.

The flowers generally fall into three types: perennial, annual and biennial, and bulbs, and it is best to have separate beds for each within your growing area. To fill this sort of area you will need in the region of 40 perennial plants and 80 annuals and biennials. Bear in mind that you will be planting them closer together than you would in an ornamental garden – you want to reduce the amount of bare soil to a minimum to help suppress any weed growth. The number of bulbs will depend on whether you want to grow dahlias too, which take up quite a lot of space but are well worth growing.

DECIDING WHAT FLOWERS TO GROW

The chances are that you will want to grow flowers that you like – and if you like them, so will other people. Remember, however, that it is important to have as long a cutting season as possible so don't pick ones that all flower within a period of six weeks in the summer! Below is a selection that I like; they cover a long flowering period and have been popular with my friends – and they are easy to grow.

A number of them may be grown as dual-purpose plants because they can also be used for dyeing – particularly achillea, rudbeckia and solidago, tubers and bulbs such as dahlia and narcissus, and some foliage plants like eucalyptus. Some of the flowers could be used as an 'extra' in soap making, if you fancy trying your hand at this (see Chapter 11), such as calendula and centaurea petals, or pounded eucalyptus leaves.

Perennials

Listed here are perennials that I wouldn't be without: between them they provide flowers from spring through to autumn.

Achillea sp. – Achillea should be cut when all the flowers on the inflorescence are open, otherwise they will droop.

Ammi sp. – There are two species which are ideal for cutting: the more common *Ammi majus*, and *A. visnaga*. Both resemble cow parsley, although *A. visnaga* has 'lacier' foliage but 'chunkier' flowers than *A. majus*. They are both really good 'filler' flowers in a bunch.

Delphinium – No cutting garden should be without delphiniums. I prefer the cultivars with looser, single flowers, especially the 'Belladonna' hybrids, rather than the tightly packed, or double ones, like the 'Pacific Giants' range.

Echinacea purpurea – As well as looking lovely, echinacea have a very long flowering season which makes them ideal for cutting. In addition to the usual pink/purple variety you can now get shades of yellow too.

Eryngium sp. – I have found the best variety to be *E. planum*; its flowers are small, its stems are blue and it will go well with every other flower in the bunch.

Euphorbia sp. – There are many varieties to choose from and each makes a really good 'filler' flower. The early flowering *E. amygdaloides* var. *robbiae* and the late flowering *E. schillingii* are two of the best. A word of warning: the euphorbia sap can irritate the skin, so be careful when you cut it. Plunge the cut stems into boiling water for a few seconds and the sap will stop flowing.

Gaura lindheimeri – This plant has a very long flowering season so it is ideal for cutting.

Lysimachia atropurpurea 'Beaujolais' – This is a lovely 'cut and come again' flower which has spikes of deep red flowers.

Paeonia lactiflora – Peonies take a while to become established and large enough plants from which to cut flowers but it is worth the wait. Five blooms in a bunch can command a premium price.

Phlox paniculata – These flowers will last for ages in a vase. Be sure to look for varieties that are advertised as mildew resistant.

Rudbeckia sp. – These flowers are often mistaken for echinacea. They have a similar daisy-like flower form and share the same common name of cone flower so perhaps it's not surprising.

Scabiosa caucasica – These are real 'cottage garden' favourites and make excellent cut flowers.

Solidago sp. – This is the ubiquitous 'golden rod' which you either love or hate. Either way, it makes a good cut flower, so is worth including in your cutting bed. Beware, though, it can become invasive, so keep and eye on it.

Verbena bonariensis – Although technically a perennial it is very short-lived and many people grow it as an annual. Either way, its airy inflorescences are lovely for cutting.

Bulbs

I have included corms and tubers as well as bulbs here. Spring-flowering bulbs are indispensable for cutting: they are available before just about any other sort of flower and combined with some evergreen foliage make a spectacular display. And don't forget the bulbs, corms and tubers that flower at other times of the year. Three or five stems can give any bunch a real focal point – especially ones like alliums or dahlias.

Allium sp. – These are members of the onion family, and some of them do have an onion fragrance about them. Nevertheless, they are worth growing for their beautiful, spherical flowers. Look out for *A. giganteum*, *A. hollandicum* 'Purple Sensation', and *A. sphaerocephalon* in particular.

Dahlia sp. – These are almost obligatory in any cutting garden. If you keep picking them they will reward you with even more flowers, and they last right until the first frosts. Search out some of the more unusual or brighter colours – they will add a real dynamism to your bunch.

Gladiolus sp. – Forget a certain Dame Edna, they make a lovely addition to any bunch, especially the more dainty-flowered *G. communis* subsp. *byzantinus* which blooms earlier than the large-flowered hybrids.

Narcissus sp. – An essential addition to the spring bouquet.

Nerine bowdenii – This beautiful bulbous perennial blooms in late autumn when lots of other flowers are well past their best.

Tulipa – Tulips are perhaps the most opulent of all spring bulbs; with their varying jewel-like colours and their differing forms they can make a show-stopping display. They will continue to grow after cutting and tend to be somewhat lax in their habit, flopping all over the place, so after you cut them it is as well to wrap the bunches in paper to hold them straight as you condition them (conditioning is placing the cut flowers in clean water for several hours in a cool place).

Annuals and biennials

Always include some annuals and biennials in your flower mix. A good number of these tend to be more flamboyant in both form and colour, simply because they have to advertise themselves without reticence to pollinating insects. And they tend to be prolific flowerers for the same reason – if you cut the blooms before they have been pollinated, the plant will work overtime producing more in order to safeguard its survival as a species. Below is a small selection of 'worthies' that earn their growing space, but you may have your own favourites.

Anethum graveolens – This is dill, the herb most often grown for its foliage, but it bears lovely umbels of acid-green flowers.

Antirrhinum sp. – Snapdragons are one of the first flowers that spring to mind when you think of the quintessential cottage garden so are a must-have in any garden flower bouquet.

Calendula officinalis – The varying orangey shades of pot marigold look stunning when teamed with acid green foliage.

Centaurea cyanus – To my mind you can't beat the 'original' blue cornflower, but you can now get pinks, white and even a dark, crimson-black variety.

Cerinthe major 'Purpurascens' – I know of no other flower that goes so well with anything else you put it with: it complements every other colour.

Cosmos bipinnatus – These lovely white or pink single daisy-like flowers are lovely in their own right, but the stems also sport delicate fern-like foliage.

Dianthus barbatus – This is good old-fashioned scented sweet william. Although technically a biennial, I have found that by cutting the flowers the plant will bloom for another season without loss of vigour.

Digitalis purpurea – Be sure to cut foxgloves when at least a third of the flowers on the spike are open, otherwise you may find that they are reluctant to make an appearance.

Erysimum cheiri – Wallflowers, like *Dianthus barbatus*, are somehow thought of as relics from a bygone age but they are still every bit as valuable as cut flowers as they ever were.

Helianthus annuus – Rather than growing the giant, rather unwieldy, sunflowers I would go for the shorter-stemmed varieties like 'Lemon Sorbet' (a pale yellow variety with a branching habit so you get more than one flower on each main stem) or 'Pastiche' (which has a range of more muted colours including yellow, red and buff).

Hesperis matronalis – This is sweet rocket; not to be confused with the rocket you eat. Technically it is a biennial, but it seeds itself so readily that it acts as an annual. It is very early flowering and is one of the few cutting flowers that will grow well in the shade.

Lathyrus odoratus – Sweet peas are the cut flower *par excellence*: whole books have been written about this lovely flower. Make sure you choose scented varieties – there are some hybrids that are totally devoid of fragrance, which to my mind defeats the object of growing them.

Moluccella laevis – Otherwise known as bells of Ireland, these stems of bright green 'bells' are one of the best 'foliage' flowers there are.

Nicotiana sp. – Various species of tobacco plant make ideal flowers for cutting, as long as you opt for the longer-stemmed varieties.

Nigella sp. – There are two species of Nigella that are worth growing: *N. damascena*, which produces white, pink or the usual blue flowers, and *N. hispanica*, which has larger, deeper blue flowers.

Zinnia sp. – This has to be one of my favourite flowers for cutting: they look lovely massed together in a single bunch but look equally as good in a mixed offering. They are half-hardy, so don't be in too much of a rush to sow the seeds in the spring.

Foliage plants

Don't forget to grow some foliage plants: a good selection of foliage will complement the flowers in a bunch beautifully. Many of the more 'feathery' flowers will also give some foliage effect, too.

Asparagus – You can have your cake (or foliage) and eat it too with asparagus! Cut the tender young spears for six weeks as they appear early in the season (either eat them yourself, or sell them) and thereafter leave the shoots to develop into foliage for cutting. As long as you only cut half the growth there will be enough foliage for the plant to shore up its reserves for next year.

Eucalyptus – Forget the towering trees of Australia: by cutting the stems back regularly you will not only keep it in check but be provided with an abundance of grey, rounded foliage.

Salix – Pussy willow is ideal to cut early in the year and one of the most dramatic is *Salix* x *savensis* which also has red-coloured bark.

GROWING YOUR FLOWERS

I have assumed that you have enough knowledge to plant, grow and look after your flower plants, and there are numerous excellent books on the market to help you. It is worth calling attention to a few points, however.

Weeds

The less time you spend weeding, the more time you have to grow flowers! It perhaps goes without saying that you will make sure your flower bed is free of perennial weeds before you start planting it. One useful way to reduce the number of weeds that will be determined to infiltrate your newly cultivated beds is to mulch, mulch and mulch again. This will keep the weeds at bay but also help to retain moisture.

Staking

Judicious staking is always worthwhile, although you may find that if you plant closely enough the plants will support each other. You are aiming for straight-stemmed flowers, so if in doubt, stake.

Watering

Unless the weather is really hot, perennials and bulbs should not need watering, especially if you have got your soil right to begin with. Annuals need watering until they are established, and perhaps extra water thereafter. This is because there is no need for their root systems to develop to the same extent as perennials – annuals only live for one season – and they will not be able to draw on deep-seated moisture reserves in the way that perennials can. So think about irrigation before you start planting and grow those flowers that are likely to need watering as close to the water source as possible.

CUTTING YOUR FLOWERS

This is probably the most important part. It is one thing to grow beautiful flowers but you want to cut them off in their prime – literally – and still make them look beautiful. Timing is the key, in terms of at what stage in the flower's life you cut it, and at what time of day.

When should you cut your flowers?

The flower is a plant's reproduction mechanism. It is there to attract pollinating insects, and after pollination the seed will grow and the flower itself will die away. So if your flower is showing loose pollen it is too late to cut it – it will have a very short vase-life.

Most species can be cut in the bud stage, as long as there is some petal colour showing, or just when the petals have begun to unfurl. Dahlias are the exception – only cut these when they are fully open, but before the pollen starts to loosen. Spiky flowers, like delphiniums, should be cut when about a quarter of the flowers towards the base of the spike are open.

What time of day should you cut your flowers?

Morning or evening? A much debated point. Some people advocate cutting flowers in the morning because that is when they are most turgid. Others say that you should cut them in the evening because they have had all day to photosynthesize, have built up their store of carbohydrate and will therefore last longer in the vase.

If you cut in the morning be sure to do it after any dew has dried (any moisture left on the leaves and flowers can promote fungus) and before it gets too hot. If you cut in the evening, wait until it is cool. The choice is yours.

I like to cut in the evening because I can then give the flowers a good long drink overnight – known as conditioning, a practice that you should adopt when cutting any flowers. Then in the morning I can arrange them for myself or bunch them up for friends. If you plan to sell at farmers' markets, this method is perhaps the best because you won't have time to cut, condition, and bunch your flowers on the same morning as you intend to sell them.

Equipment

Equipment is straightforward – you need something sharp with which to cut your flowers, and something in which to put them. A pair of secateurs is needed for cutting woody and thick-stemmed material, and I also find a pair of fruit and flower snips invaluable – they are stronger than scissors but not as hefty as secateurs. All your cutting tools must be kept scrupulously clean as any bacteria will soon multiply; you will shorten the life of your cut flowers and spread disease among your plants. You will need a number of buckets; they don't have to be fancy, but they too must be kept clean.

BUNCHING YOUR FLOWERS

There are no hard and fast rules about what flowers you should put together. I have found that many people who grow flowers have a good eye for colour, shape and texture anyway, and you will soon develop a feeling for what works and what doesn't in colour, shape and texture.

Colour

Monochrome bunches work well, as do combinations of complementary colours, like blue and orange. But experiment: combine colours like magenta and orange with acid green – it has a certain zing about it!

Shape and texture

Don't forget different shapes and textures. Combine 'flat' flowers with 'fluffy' ones, and 'silky' ones with 'spiky' ones until you have a pleasing mix.

Size of bunches

How much you put in a bunch will depend on who you are giving them to or selling them to. You can be generous with friends, but don't be too generous if you are selling them – you want to make some money! Put several different-sized bunches together, priced accordingly, and see what sells. You will soon get a feel for what your customers like.

WRAPPING YOUR FLOWERS

Florists' flowers tend to be wrapped in cellophane, which protects them but also adds to the feel of opulence, especially if combined with a layer of colour-coordinated tissue paper. The bouquets are nearly always tied with a coloured ribbon and flouncy bow.

Because your flowers come from the garden you might like to try a more rustic and environmentally friendly alternative, such as brown paper tied with raffia. It is really up to you. Whatever you choose it is a good idea to give your flowers some sort of protection when your customers buy them.

Consider giving some care information with your flowers – what to do when you get them home and so on. A label tied to the bunch with instructions on one side and your name on the other is a good way of getting any information to your customers, as well as reminding them who they bought the flowers from. A luggage label is ideal for this, especially if you are adopting a more rustic feel for your wrapping material.

AND FINALLY . . .

Don't forget that growing flowers is a seasonal enterprise. Even if you expand your season by a few weeks by growing some flowers under cover in a greenhouse or polytunnel, you will only have blooms, and therefore income, from spring through to the autumn. (I am assuming that you would not be heating your greenhouse.) There will be plenty of maintenance work to do during this time, of course, but you will have time to reflect on the previous year and to plan any improvements or changes to your range of flowers. And you should have time to put your feet up, too!

CASE STUDY – ANDREA JONES

Returning from a holiday in New Zealand in April 2008, Andrea Jones was astounded at the vibrant spring growth that had appeared in the six weeks she had been away. She wondered why we don't make more use of abundant British flowers and foliage to mark the gradual change of seasons and celebrate what is available, instead of resorting to the relatively narrow choice of florists' flowers that are available all year round. We are gradually becoming more aware of the benefits of buying local and seasonal food, so why not do the same with flowers?

And so Andrea's business seed was set, which has now blossomed into a growing enterprise. She aims for beautiful flowers, locally and sustainably grown and with scent where possible – she pointed out that even roses in a bouquet aren't bred for scent these days. She now has a vast range of flowers and foliage selected for the climatic conditions in her area (Ayrshire, Scotland) and is currently using her own small garden and a couple of other gardens which have become her cutting patches.

From April to October a mixture of perennials, bulbs and shrubs provide her with ever-changing combinations of flowers and foliage on a week-by-week basis, reflecting the seasonal changes of spring to summer to autumn. 'These happily grow themselves without much coaxing from me,' she says, making it sound deceptively simple!

She also grows many biennials and annuals to increase the selection and yield of flowers available each season. Choosing the best varieties for cutting, harvesting at the right time and proper post-harvest treatment gives her five to seven days or more on vase-life (depending on the variety), making locally grown flowers a viable option.

Andrea has gardened organically throughout her life, learning from her parents, so her cutting garden was naturally going to be managed organically. She told me that this was especially important to her because the conventional cut flower industry uses vast quantities of artificial fertilizers, herbicides and pesticides to produce stock high in yield, uniformity and resilient to global transportation by air.

'Most cut flower consumers seem unaware of these production methods,' she says. 'People don't seem to be as concerned because flowers are not eaten, but their production nevertheless has a great environmental impact, especially in the developing world, and in my view is not sustainable.' She goes on to explain that this globalized production also limits the range of flowers that are available. 'People who buy my flowers love the fact that they can't get such varieties or scent elsewhere and my flowers seem unusual or unique and they don't cost the earth.'

Andrea mainly sells mixed bunches, picked and arranged to order through word of mouth and via her website (www.mayfieldflowers.co.uk). 'I enjoy the very personal service I can give, although as the grower, marketeer and arranger it can feel a bit like a labour of love doing all aspects myself!' She says that brides are very interested in 'eco friendly' weddings or seek out locally grown flowers as an alternative to the more traditional wedding styles. 'Being able to say that someone is growing your wedding flowers for you offers a level of individuality that people often look for to mark their wedding day.'

I asked Andrea what it was about her business that she enjoyed most. 'I love being outside, in tune with the seasons, and growing such a range of beautiful flowers which I can then use to create my own style of arrangements.' Andrea's flowers are truly beautiful and the arrangements stunning. I am inspired enough to think that I might just have to expand my own cutting patch.

PART 3

Food and Drink

Introduction

In Part 1 we looked at chickens, goats and bees and in Part 2 we discovered the delights of herbs, soft fruit and flowers. Now we turn our attention to how we can use some of the fruits of our labour. We don't necessarily have to eat the produce straight away or even store it; we can turn it into other products – especially ones to eat and drink. For example, milk from goats can be used to make cheese; eggs from chickens are a main ingredient in lemon curd; you can't make mead without honey, which can also be included in many preserves; herbs can find their way into preserves and cheese; and fruit makes delicious jams.

So in this part we explore making these things – cheese, sweet preserves, and cider and mead – and show how we can 'add value' to the basic products, either to share between friends and family, or to sell and generate a little income.

CHAPTER 7

MAKING CHEESE

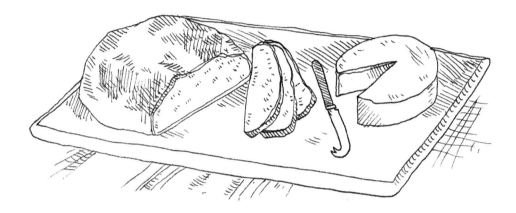

Every great meal can be topped off by the great cheese selection. A good cheese board will sing out your taste and qualities as much as your love for your guests. And what better a way than to show them you care than by including a selection of your own home-made cheeses?

Space does not permit the section I would have liked to include on the history of cheese. The abridged version is thus: the production of cheese is very old and can be found in a variety of cultures and regions.

WHAT IS CHEESE?

Nowadays, cheese is a generic term for a group of food products. Cheese is so widely known and varied that you can no longer describe it as just cheese. It demands refinement such as a locality (Cornwall, Cheshire, Wensleydale); type of milk (goat, sheep, buffalo); or process (river-washed, smoked, blue-veined). And even then all is not as it seems. Cheddar, for example, is not considered to be from a locality, but is a generic 'type'. You can buy cheddars from many different parts of the world but none of them has glimpsed Somerset!

Most cheese that you buy in mainstream shops is made from cow's milk but cheese made from sheep or goat's milk is becoming increasingly available. They have a rich taste, and are also bought for their apparent health-giving properties. The idea of cheese made from milk other than cow's never appealed to me, until I was offered a meal of cheese, cubed, fried and served with salad. I didn't know that it was made from a mix of sheep, goat and cow's milk but it was delicious and now I can't get enough of it. I love the squeak it leaves on your teeth.

What is cheese made from?

Cheese is made from milk, but more precisely, the proteins and fats present in milk. Cheese is made by the coagulation of the milk protein, casein. Without being too scientific, the milk is acidified and the addition of the enzyme rennet (or similar product) causes the bulk to coagulate. The solids are then separated and pressed into its final form. Sounds really simple, doesn't it? There's a little bit more to it than that, but let's look first at what you need in a little more detail.

Milk

As we said above, you can use different types of milk to make cheese: cow, sheep, goat, buffalo – in theory, any lactating animal will provide milk from which you can make cheese.

Starter culture

The starter culture contains the bacteria required to ensure that the milk is at the maximum level of acidity before it is turned into curds (the solids) and whey (the liquid). Several different strains of starter culture are available; the one you choose depends on the types of cheese you are going to produce. The most common cultures are *Streptococcus lactis* and *Streptococcus cremoris*.

Some starters are suitable for different types of cheese, such as both soft and pressed cheeses, while others are specifically designed for a particular cheese. Some are used for a mix that requires a higher temperature; these are known as thermophilic. Swiss and Italian cheeses need this type, as they require greater heat when being processed. A general all-round starter is known as mesophilic and works at a low temperature.

When you have decided what sort of cheese you will be making you can choose your starter accordingly. Your starter kit will usually arrive foil-wrapped and freeze-dried. Keep it in the freezer until you are ready to use it.

Rennet

Rennet, in essence, is a fast-acting curdling agent. It works against the milk protein casein; the rennet causes separation of the milk into curds and whey. Traditional rennet is made from calf's stomach, but usually the 'rennet' you get these days is a vegetable derivative, suitable for all.

As a general rule, 4 drops of rennet are required per 5 litres of milk for a soft cheese; and 4 drops per 1 litre of milk for a hard cheese. The exact amounts can be fine-tuned depending on the 'style' of cheese you are looking for. Keep a record of how much you have used each time you make a batch, so that when you hit on 'the one' you will have a chance of replicating it next time. Some cheese makers take years to get this right, so don't be disappointed if things don't go to plan straight away.

Salt

Salt enhances the flavour of the product and acts as a preservative. It also helps to drain residual liquid from the cheese so it will firm up. The precise amounts per cheese and type of cheese will obviously vary, but generally speaking for dry salting the ratio is 2% per kilo of curds; if you are using a brine solution, it is 20% brine (200ml of salt per litre of water).

Additions

Some cheese makers like to spice up their cheeses – some literally. By adding spices or crushed black peppercorns a cheese can be transformed. Herbs such as chives can be used too. When making a hard cheese these items are usually added prior to the cheeses being pressed and settled.

CASE STUDY – MARTIN AND KATE RUSSELL

Martin and Kate Russell run Turnover Farm in Hampshire. Martin's family have farmed there for over 400 years; they have mainly dairy cattle and use a small proportion of their milk for cheese. The family-run farm is home to a number of goats and sheep as well, and their milk is also used for cheese. They are thinking about having more goats and sheep because of the increasing demand for this particular type of milk and cheese.

Martin works his cows on the beautiful grasslands of Hampshire. The majority of the milk is sold on and only a small amount retained for making cheese. His grandfather started the interest in cheese making but Martin has made it into a cottage industry.

The Russells produce small quantities of two types of cheese: a yellow, slightly hard cheese, akin to Wensleydale or a creamy Lancashire, and a beautiful brie, stunningly rich and creamy, which they sometimes flavour with lavender from their own herb bed. Because they make only limited amounts of cheese, it is select in many ways.

When I asked them where they saw the future of the farm, quick as a flash they said cheese, especially the lavender brie.

Martin took me through the Russell family cheese-making process, keeping it as simple as possible.

HOW DO YOU MAKE CHEESE?

Pasteurization

Most milk from supermarkets is already pasteurized but you need to heat the milk to kill off any unwanted bacteria that might harm the cheese-making process. The milk should be heated to 66°C and held there for 30 minutes, then allowed to cool to about 21°C. Two teaspoons of the milk is put to one side – it is used to mix with the rennet later.

The starter

Martin uses what is known as a traditional 'incubated before use' starter, which means that he has to prepare it beforehand. He suggested that someone just beginning to make their own cheese would be advised to use a DVI, or direct vat inoculation, which requires you to sprinkle the contents of the packet onto the milk, and there you are!

The starter is stirred in and the pasteurized milk is covered and left in a warm place for about an hour to acidify. Martin has a 'warming cupboard' but it could be placed next to a radiator or an Aga, or by the fire, or even in the airing cupboard. It should not be left too long, though, as the cheese mix will become dry and crumbly.

Adding the rennet

Martin mixed a few drops of rennet with the two teaspoons of milk that had been set aside earlier. To this he added a small amount of cool, but not cold, water.

Next he warmed the milk, complete with starter, to 30°C. This is the correct temperature for cow's milk; if it had been goat's milk the temperature required would be 28°C. The milk mixture was then taken off the heat and the rennet mixture added and stirred in.

The mixture should then be given a good five minutes to rest before being stirred again, as the cream rises to the surface. After another stir to incorporate any cream, it is covered and left to set in a warm place. Again, Martin used his warming cupboard but any warm place will do, as long as it is not too hot – you don't want to cook your milk mixture.

Setting/coagulation

The mix will settle down and start to coagulate. You can tell when it is ready for the next stage because there will be a resistance when you touch it and there won't be a milky mark left on your finger. Martin uses rennet that is suitable for vegetarians – this type of rennet takes longer to 'set' than the traditional rennet, so you have to be a patient.

Scoring or cutting the curd

When the curd has settled to a point where it is semi-solid you need cut it to release the liquid, or whey. With expert ease Martin whipped out a knife and eased the curd away from the sides of the container, sliced the curd left to right, up and down, and back and forwards, leaving the mix with evenly spaced blocks of curd. With another knife – his curd knife – he cut the blocks of curd into much smaller pieces. He then gently stirred these pieces with his hand without breaking them up any more.

'Cooking' the curd

At this point the temperature of the curds and whey is raised very slowly to 38°C – this should take place over a period of about 30 minutes, during which time the curds need a gentle stir with your hands periodically.

Pitching

When the required temperature was reached Martin took to stirring the curds vigorously so that the curds dropped to the bottom of the pan and collected in the middle. He then turned off the heat and left the pan until the contents were quite still.

Draining the whey away

At this point as much of the liquid whey as possible needs to drained away. Martin started by ladling out what he could without disturbing the curds too much. He then got a sterilized cloth (it looked like an old linen tablecloth) and draped it over the top of a stainless steel bucket. Then he tipped in the curds, making sure that they stayed in the cloth and didn't spill over into the bucket. After the curds had drained a little, he tied the corners of the cloth together and lifted the bundle onto a baking tray. With an upturned spoon placed underneath the tray to raise it at one end, allowing any excess whey to run off, this was left for around 15 minutes.

Texturing, stacking or cheddaring

What you call this process depends on where you are in the country, it seems. In Hampshire Martin refers to it as stacking. He untied the bundle of curds, which had collected together to form a mass. Martin cut this mass into four slices and stacked them one on top of another. The whole thing was then covered with a cloth – the cloth you have just taken the curd from can be used. He waited about another 15 minutes and then moved the outer slices of the curd to the inside of the stack, and covered it again. After another 15 minutes this process was repeated. He carried on doing this until the slices had 'fused' together.

Milling and salting

Having spent all that effort stacking the curd, it was now time to cut it up into small pieces again. This is to allow salt to be incorporated into the cheese. Martin sprinkled salt over the pea-sized pieces and gently 'shuffled' them so that each piece came into contact with some salt.

Moulding

This has nothing to do with the mould that is added to cheeses like Danish Blue or Stilton. It is the process of putting the curd into a mould which has been lined with a piece of sterilized cheesecloth. Martin made a neat job of lining the mould, making sure that it was a snug fit. You may think this is fairly straightforward but not all moulds are circular, like the ones that Martin uses. He has tried using square moulds but they don't give the traditional shape that his customers look for.

He added the curd to the mould, pushing it down until the mould was full. The remainder of the cheesecloth was folded over the top of the curd.

Pressing

Once in the mould the cheese needs to be pressed to compact the curds and at the same time express the remaining whey. Martin placed what he called a follower on top of the mould, a flat piece of wood that would help distribute the weight of the press evenly over the cheese. Then the mould complete with follower went into the press and he applied a little pressure. You don't want too much pressure immediately; at first you have to be quite gentle, so that you don't lose the fats in the cheese along with the whey.

After an hour or so he increased the pressure to maximum and it stayed like this for 24 hours. At this stage Martin always says a prayer to the god of cheese, or so he said. I was really impressed, but then he burst into giggles. I'm so gullible.

I wasn't around to see the rest of the process, so he explained what would happen next over a plate of scones, complete with clotted cream and strawberry jam (all home-made, of course).

The next day the pressure is released, the cheese taken out of the mould and the cloth replaced with a new one. The cheese is then put back in the mould, but the other way up, and the pressing process is repeated.

Drying or airing

Then the cheese is removed from the press and the cloth taken off. It will now be recognizable as cheese. It is dipped into water heated to 66°C for at least a minute to remove any scaring, fluff or uneven surfaces. You want a nice smooth surface. Then the cheese is placed in what Martin calls his holding area, which is kept at 18–21°C, for a couple of days until he sees a rind forming. This is just the ghost of a rind not a thick one.

Sealing the cheese

After the rind is formed the cheese has to be sealed to prevent it being damaged, to help preserve it and to stop it from drying out too much.

A number of products are used to seal cheese. Some cheese makers will use a bandage, others a thinner form of cheesecloth; one of the most common ways of sealing is to use wax. This wax is available from a number of home product retailers either in shops or online and comes in a variety of colours. I know a cheese maker in Lancashire who uses a black wax to highlight the depth, strength and maturity of the cheese.

Martin uses a very natural wax. He uses bees' wax from my hives, melts it, strains it and filters it, and dips his cheeses into that. It not only suits their cheese, it adds a slight flavour, which is a really good selling point.

You may be wondering how you can coat a cheese without leaving a fingerprint. You can use a brush and do one side at a time, but this will need at least two coats. Or you can use a wax 'bath'; this isn't a specialist piece of equipment – it can be a bowl over a pan of hot water to produce a bain marie, or just a pan of hot wax. If you dip by hand you still have the fingerprint issue, although the wax does set very quickly. Some cheese makers use a small piece of wire, almost like a thin basket, but with this method the cheese still has to be dipped twice, one half covered at a time and left to set. Martin uses a piece of wire that passes through the cheese and is bent outwards on the base to support the cheese. After dipping the cheeses are hung up to dry.

Maturing

Maturing is the final stage and a very, very important one. If you were to open your cheese a day after dipping, it would not be fresh or light in flavour – it would be bland and almost tasteless. If you had incorporated herbs, spice or peppercorns into it, all you would taste is the flavour of the additions suspended in a bland cheese-y mass. Cheese is left to mature so that it becomes full of flavour and any additions complement the full flavour of the cheese rather than overpower it. Imagine a Double Gloucester with its tangy flavour and expressive colour with a just hint of chives, garlic or thyme just resting behind its cheese flavour. Lovely.

You need to leave cheese to mature in a cool, dry area. Martin has a special room; what you need is a dry area with a constant temperature of 8–11°C.

The cheese needs to be turned daily for the first three weeks and then every other day after that. Be patient – even a small cheese will take at least a month to mature; large ones need around three months to produce even a mild cheese. For a strong mature cheese that makes your eyes water you may have to wait for a year.

Once your cheese has reached the level of maturity that you want, the best way to store it until you want to eat it is to cut it into portions and freeze it. Many people are unaware that you can freeze cheese: wrapped well it will keep for several months. Be sure to keep it away from any strong-smelling items in your freezer, though; the last thing you want is your precious cheese smelling more of kippers than cheese.

MAKING COTTAGE CHEESE

If the rigmarole of making your own hard cheese is not for you, there are other cheeses you can make in a very short time with the minimum amount of fuss and ingredients but with the maximum amount of flavour. Making your own soft cheeses, such as paneer or cottage cheese, or even a tasty yogurt, is straightforward. A freshly made cottage cheese, chilled, served on your own home-made rye bread, home-made butter and some snips of your own home-grown chives, is a delight! So here is a really simple recipe for cottage cheese.

Cottage cheese recipe

You will need:

    2 pints (1.2 litres) skimmed or semi-skimmed milk
    2 tablespoons (30ml) lemon juice or white vinegar
    Pinch of salt

Pour the milk into a stainless steel saucepan and, stirring occasionally, heat it until it is very hot, but not boiling.

Take it off the heat and allow it to cool for just a couple of minutes before adding the lemon juice or vinegar.

Stir it gently and you will see the milk separating into curds and whey.

Allow the mixture to cool and then pour it through a sieve, allowing the whey to collect in a bowl underneath. You can use this later to make scones.

Put the curds into a bowl and sprinkle with the salt. At this stage you can add some chopped chives or pepper – anything you like really. And there you have it!

Whey

I've suggested using the whey in scones – just add instead of milk. But if you have a lot of whey and you keep pigs or you know someone who does, offer it to the porkers – they will love it!

CASE STUDY – GILL PATEMAN

Martin and Kate Russell run their cheese-making enterprise on a small scale. Gill Pateman, of Merlin Cheeses, set deep in the Welsh countryside, gives us an idea of what making cheese on a larger, but still artisan, level is like.

Gill's interest in making cheese grew out of a family necessity. In 1979 Gill's daughter Rebecca developed an allergy to cow's milk. Gill already had a smallholding, so it wasn't long before Sara the goat moved in and started producing milk for Rebecca. In due course along came Stella, Sian and Susan, Sara's kids, who when the time came were milked as well. Gill ended up with a 'goat's milk lake' and as she explained, 'the family were getting sick of rice puddings and egg custards every mealtime!' So she turned her hand to making cheese.

At first Gill made cheese just for family, friends and neighbours but as she was looking for ways to make an income from the smallholding in 1986 she took the plunge into making cheese to sell commercially. She invested in more milking goats, and cheese-making equipment. By 1998 the business had built up to such an extent that she had a milking herd of over 200 goats.

Later she started buying in local goat's milk and reduced the number of goats she milked herself; by 2005 she had stopped using her own goat's milk to concentrate fully on cheese-making. This coincided with the building of purpose-built, high-grade food production premises with cheese-making, packing and storage facilities.

Up until 2008 Gill produced only goat's milk cheddar, but she has since extended the range to include cheddars made with cow's and buffalo milk. In all she now has over three dozen varieties, all of them reflecting the brand name. For example, as well as the 'Merlin' range there is the 'Arthurian' collection, which includes the names of Lancelot, Mordred and Galahad, and Guinevere and Morgana – the names alone make you want to try them!

Merlin Cheeses is a real family affair – all five of Gill's children have been involved at one time or another. She also employs people part-time and when it's really busy she takes on students to help out. Gill sells her cheeses throughout the UK, through wholesalers, retailers and by mail order. She also attends food fairs, which she says are a vital outlet: 'By attending food fairs and meeting our customers new and old we are able to continuously improve and develop our cheeses according to what people like,' she explains.

Gill runs a truly successful business but she is modest about her achievement, which started on such a small scale. 'When I began making cheese it was because of necessity, having to do something with the excess milk we had. I got various cheese-making books from the library and I just experimented and learnt from my successes as well as my failures.' Gill's enterprise is a living embodiment of the saying that 'great oaks from little acorns grow' – or should it be 'big cheeses from little truckles'?

CHAPTER 8

MAKING SWEET PRESERVES

The process of preserving foodstuffs has been practised for millennia. Nowadays we have the refrigerator and freezer which have revolutionized the way we shop, and preserve foodstuffs, but perhaps the oldest method of preserving, and one still carried out today, is that of drying. Sun-dried tomatoes are an almost 'must-have' item in the store cupboard nowadays, and where would Christmas cake be without currants, raisins and sultanas (all dried grape varieties)? Freezing and canning, too, provide means of preserving food.

Most people, however, associate the term 'preserving' with making things like jams, chutneys and pickles, and indeed these are some of the most interesting ways of giving produce 'added value' or providing an attractive addition to the meal table. It also takes advantage of using seasonal produce, especially if you have a glut. You can, of course, freeze a good number of fruit and vegetables, but there is something altogether more satisfying in transforming all those punnets of raspberries into a delicious jam so that you can have a taste of high summer in the depths of winter.

Inspired by the previous sections in this book you may be tempted to try your hand at growing soft fruits or herbs, or keeping bees or chickens. You may find that it is more profitable to 'add value' to some of your end results by using them in a product that can demand a higher return, and have a longer 'shelf-life' than the original (the exception being honey, which will keep for many years without any intervention). So in this chapter we look at making sweet preserves like jams, curds and jellies, in which we can use some of the items produced in previous chapters, like honey, eggs, soft fruits and herbs. A number of recipes are included.

WHAT PRESERVING DOES

In a nutshell, the various methods of preserving kill off harmful micro-organisms which can spoil food and pose a risk to our health. The preserves that we shall concentrate on employ a number of factors to achieve this.

First, heat: enzymes and yeasts are destroyed at temperatures above 60°C; moulds and fungi above 88°C; bacteria at 100°C. (The setting point of jam is 104.5°C which immediately takes care of any baddies.) Second, the use of a high concentration of a preserving medium, such as sugar, for sweet preserves. Third, the exclusion of air, which means well-sealed jars.

It almost goes without saying that good hygiene – food, kitchen and personal – is essential so that you start with a scrupulously clean environment and equally clean equipment.

THE EQUIPMENT YOU'LL NEED

Before we can start making any sort of preserve we need some basic equipment. This will involve a fairly modest initial monetary outlay but once you have these items they will last almost a lifetime and you will find that they are indispensable.

PRESERVING PAN, OR MASLIN PAN

Originally preserving pans were made from a mixture of metals, hence the name maslin, which means 'composed of different materials', but nowadays they are mostly made of stainless steel. (Avoid aluminium, which can react with the acid content of fruits.) Get hold of a robust one with a capacity of about 9 litres, with a good, strong handle.

ACCURATE SCALES

Accurate scales are vital for weighing out ingredients. If you are selling your preserves to the public you may need 'certified' retail scales to weigh your final product – check with your Trading Standards Officer.

SUGAR THERMOMETER

This is essential if you want to take the guesswork out of jam and especially curd making. The crucial temperatures are marked on the thermometer.

WOODEN SPOONS

Forget the weedy ones you get for creaming butter and sugar together – you need big, 'man-size' spoons for preserve making. Keep your spoons solely for making sweet preserves – if you use them for any other purpose they will inevitably become infused with other flavours which you really don't want transferred to your jams or jellies.

OTHER SPOONS

A slotted spoon is useful for skimming scum, and a ladle always comes in handy.

MEASURING JUG

A measuring jug is essential for measuring liquids. Heat-resistant ones are best as you can use these for pouring preserves into jars.

SIEVE

You will need a sieve if your recipe calls for pureed ingredients. Make sure that you have a nylon sieve – metal could react with acidic ingredients.

FUNNEL

Not an essential item, but a funnel is very useful for filling jars.

JELLY BAG AND STAND

This is only needed if you intend to make jellies. Purpose-made bags and stands are fairly inexpensive and are far better than any improvised Heath Robinson affair that you can rig up with a stool and muslin.

Jars

You will need lidded jars. If you are making preserves purely for your own consumption you can use waxed discs and cellophane covers, secured with an elastic band – my mum and gran always used this method. If you intend to offer your preserves to the public you will probably be required to use jars with twist-on lids with a plasticized lining. These are suitable for all preserves.

SIZE OF JAR

The size of jar you use is really your choice. The majority of preserves are sold by net metric weight, usually 225g, 340g, or 450g (give or take 5g). (These are roughly equivalent to the old imperial weights of 4oz, 12oz and 1lb.) These weights can vary depending on the type of preserve, but you need to clearly display the weight on any label you use. You may also find some preserves sold by volume.

STERILIZE YOUR JARS

It is important to sterilize the jars just before you use them. This can be done in a number of ways: wash and rinse them thoroughly and put them in a low oven to dry; immerse them in a pan of cold water and bring it to the boil; or run them through the hottest dishwasher cycle. If you are making hot preserves the jars should still be warm when you fill them.

GATHERING THE RAW MATERIALS

Fruit

Always use the freshest fruit for your preserves and prepare them as appropriate for the recipe. For example, if you are making strawberry jam, hull the strawberries. Never use tainted, damaged or bruised fruit– they will spoil the entire batch.

PECTIN CONTENT OF FRUIT

Pectin is a naturally occurring substance found in all fruit. When pectin is combined with sugar and acid it forms a bond that causes jam to set. The pectin content of fruit varies, so you may have to add pectin to achieve an adequate set when using some fruits. The table gives you an idea of pectin and also acid levels in different fruits.

Commercial pectin comes in either liquid or powder form: follow the manufacturer's instructions on the packet or bottle to make sure that you use the correct amount. Alternatively you can make your own pectin stock from fruits naturally high in pectin – see recipe below.

ACID CONTENT OF FRUIT

As well as pectin, all fruits contain acid but in varying degrees. Acid draws pectin out of the fruit, which helps to achieve a more rapid set, so if the fruit you are using contains little acid, the easiest way to remedy it is to add 30ml lemon juice to each kilo of fruit you use.

Fruit	Pectin content	Acid content
Apples – cooking	High	High
Apples – crab	High	High
Apples – eating	Medium	Low
Blackberries	Low/Medium	Low
Citrus fruits	High	High
Cherries – sweet	Low	Low
Currants	High	High
Damsons	High	High
Gooseberries	High	High
Pears	Low	Low
Plums – sweet	Medium	Medium
Raspberries	Medium	Medium
Rhubarb	Low	Low
Strawberries	Low	Low

Sugar

The type of sugar you use will depend on the type of preserve you are making and, to a degree, your own personal preference. Ordinary white granulated sugar is fine for most preserves, especially jams and marmalades. I always use a fair trade variety, often golden granulated.

A specially formulated 'jam sugar', which has pectin added to it, is available, which you might like to use if the fruit you are using is low in pectin, like pears or strawberries.

Brown sugar is obviously darker and has a richer flavour, which will affect the outcome of the recipe. I only use brown sugar in savoury preserves but it could be used in marmalades if you wanted a more robust flavour.

Added extras

We are familiar with adding spices to savoury preserves but I have experimented several times with adding herbs to some of my jams. (There is a recipe below for apple, pear and lemon verbena jam.) If you grow your own herbs you could try adding some to your recipes. I wouldn't advocate introducing more than one variety, though: the extra flavours may be too overpowering, especially if you are dealing with a delicately flavoured fruit.

MAKING SWEET PRESERVES

Most sweet preserves rely on a high concentration of sugar – over 60% – to create an environment that is hostile to micro-organisms; most are also cooked to a high temperature, although there are exceptions to this. As well as sugar – and fruit, of course – sweet preserves require two more ingredients to allow them to set. These are pectin and acid.

Jam

By far the most well-known sweet preserve is jam. This is simply fruit and sugar boiled together. You can make a straightforward jam using just one kind of fruit – these are sometimes the most successful if you have a distinct or delicately flavoured fruit like strawberries – or you can use a combination of fruit and other ingredients to bring about a subtle effect, like pairing gooseberries with elderflower.

Marmalades

In effect marmalade is jam made from citrus fruits. The name marmalade comes from the Portuguese for quince, *marmelo*, which was made into a paste or jam and is still known in Portugal today as *marmelada*.

Jellies

Jellies are made by boiling strained fruit juice and sugar together to produce a clear, 'bit-free' preserve. Jellies are delicious in their own right, but you can also use an apple jelly as a base for savoury jellies containing herbs.

Curds

These are relatively low in sugar and because they also contain eggs and butter they have a very short shelf-life unless you keep them unopened in a refrigerator. For this reason alone you may not want to make curds for sale to the public. If you can find a local tea shop that will serve your curd with scones as an alternative to jam, I can almost guarantee that you will have at least one regular customer that makes the enterprise worthwhile.

UNDERSTANDING THE RULES AND REGULATIONS

If you decide to make preserves for consumption by someone other than you and your family and friends – by selling them at your local farmers' market or even supplying a local tea shop – with the idea of generating a bit of income, there are particular rules and procedures that have to be adhered to.

First of all, the place where you make your preserves has to meet certain hygiene criteria. By far the best thing to do is to contact your local Environmental Health Officer, who will be more than willing to advise you about what these criteria are and will arrange to meet you and look around your premises.

You need to be aware of what jars or containers are acceptable. You are obliged by law to put certain information on the labels, such as weight, ingredients and so on: contact your local Trading Standards Officer for help with these.

Find out about the technical differences between jams, extra jams, conserves and other preserves – these are governed by 'The Jam and Similar Products (England) Regulations 2003' which can be downloaded from the Food Standards Agency website (www.food.gov.uk).

One thing that you will undoubtedly be recommended to do is to pass the nationally recognized 'Level 2 Award Food Safety in Catering'. Courses, usually lasting just one day, are available at your local further education college. Remember, your Environmental Health Officer and Trading Standards Officer are there to help and advise you – not to try and catch you out!

RECIPES FOR YOU TO TRY

If you have been inspired by the chapters in Parts 1 and 2 to keep some livestock or grow some produce then these recipes may be just what you are looking for to add value to your 'raw materials'.

Honey can be used to replace some of the sugar in all the recipes – it will add an extra, unique dimension to your preserves, and will undoubtedly be a distinctive selling point. Do not substitute more than 15% of the sugar, though, as honey burns easily.

With these basic recipes you can make a whole range of jams, marmalades, curds and jellies. As well as using your own home-grown fruit, try experimenting with some more unusual combinations.

Jams

You can make jam from almost any kind of fruit. There are the traditional ones like strawberry or raspberry; ones that combine fruit, like blackberry and apple; and ones that are more exotic, like mango and passion fruit. I have given three recipes here, all using fruit that you can either grow yourself or is usually grown in this country. (I am not against using imported fruit to make jam but it seems to make more sense to enjoy exotic fruits fresh – we can buy them all year round nowadays.)

The first recipe is designed for strawberries and other fruit with a low pectin content such as pears and rhubarb: it can be notoriously difficult to get a good set with these fruits, hence the use of some sugar with added pectin. The second recipe can be used for any sort of fruit that has a reasonable or good pectin content, including raspberries, plums, currants and blackberries. The third contains a herb, lemon verbena, which is reminiscent of lemon sherbet – it adds a surprise element to the combination of apples and pears.

STRAWBERRY JAM

There is absolutely nothing like strawberry jam, especially when it is on top of a home-made scone with clotted cream. Strawberries are low in pectin; using some sugar with added pectin and some lemon juice helps to achieve a good set. It will always be a 'soft' set with this recipe, because of the use of honey. It makes six or seven 225g jars.

1kg strawberries, hulled and halved or quartered if they are large
500g jam sugar with pectin
325g granulated sugar
125g runny honey
150ml lemon juice

Put 200g of the strawberries into a preserving pan with 200g of the granulated sugar and squash them with a wooden spoon or potato masher. Put the pan on the hob and heat very gently until the mixture warms through. Add the rest of the strawberries and gently bring the whole lot to simmering point, making sure that the mixture doesn't catch on the bottom of the pan. Allow the mixture to simmer for about five minutes so that the fruit is slightly softened.

Add the rest of the granulated sugar and all of the jam sugar and stir gently until all the sugar has dissolved, taking care not to let the fruit break down too much, or to let it catch. When the sugar has dissolved, add the honey and lemon juice and increase the heat to bring the mixture to boiling point. Boil rapidly for about five minutes and test for setting point using a thermometer.

Remove from the heat and stir very gently if the surface is 'scummy'. Jar and seal.

JUMBLEBERRY JAM

I make this jam in the late summer or early autumn when there are lots of different fruits available. It is especially useful if you have a small amount of a number of fruits – you can jumble them up together, hence the name.

I have given the total amount of fruit that you will need; if you are using fruit that has slightly thicker skin, like blackcurrants, it is a good idea to cook them slightly in the water to soften them before you add the other fruit, lemon juice and sugar, otherwise the skins may become tough. You will need to prepare each fruit appropriately – hull strawberries, pick over blackcurrants and so on. The recipe makes six or seven 225g jars.

> 1kg fruit – I use a more or less equal mixture of strawberries,
>   raspberries and blackcurrants
> 500ml water
> Juice of 1 large lemon
> 1kg granulated sugar
> 150g runny honey

Put the fruit into a preserving pan with the water (see above) and lemon juice. Put the pan on the hob and heat very gently until the mixture warms through. Add the granulated sugar and stir gently until all the sugar has dissolved. When the sugar has dissolved, add the honey and increase the heat to bring the mixture to boiling point. Boil rapidly for about five minutes and test for setting point using a thermometer.

Remove from the heat and stir very gently if the surface is 'scummy'. Jar and seal.

PEAR, APPLE AND LEMON VERBENA JAM

I love the scent of lemon verbena, a herb I grow in my garden. This recipe came about as a result of an experiment and I hope you will agree was successful. It makes five 225g jars.

900g firm pears – I use a mixture of conference and Williams
600g cooking apples
1kg granulated sugar
150g honey
150ml lemon juice
10 leaves of lemon verbena – finely chopped

Peel and core the apples and pears and cut them into evenly sized small chunks. Put them along with all the other ingredients, except for the lemon verbena leaves, into a preserving pan and heat gently until the sugar has dissolved.

Increase the heat and boil rapidly for ten minutes or until the apples have softened. Test for setting point using a thermometer.

Remove from the heat, add the lemon verbena leaves and stir very gently to incorporate them evenly throughout the jam. Jar and seal.

Marmalade

There are basically two ways of making marmalade: the whole fruit method and the sliced fruit method.

The amount of fruit, lemon juice, granulated sugar and honey is the same for any fruit: for 1kg of fruit you need 75ml of lemon juice, 1.75kg of sugar and 250g honey. This amount will make five 450g jars.

You can make a traditional Seville orange marmalade using the bitter oranges that are available for a few short weeks in January and February, but you can use any other citrus fruit at other times of the year. Why not try lemon and lime; pink and yellow grapefruit; or my favourite, three fruit marmalade, using grapefruit, lemons and sweet oranges.

WHOLE FRUIT METHOD

This method gives a darker, cloudier result because you cook the fruits whole before cutting them into slices. First you need to scrub the fruit to remove any wax or residue, then remove the hard 'star' from the top. Put the whole fruit into a pan with 2.5 litres of water and bring to the boil. Simmer for about two hours or until the skins of the fruit can be easily pierced.

When the fruit has cooled a little, remove it from the liquid, cut each fruit in half and take out the pips. Then cut the fruit into thick, medium or thin shreds, depending on your preference, and put the whole lot back into the liquid in which it was cooked.

Add the lemon juice, sugar and honey and heat gently until the sugar has dissolved. Then boil rapidly for about five minutes and test for setting point using a thermometer. Take the pan off the heat and leave for about ten minutes, gently stir in any scum, then jar and seal.

SLICED FRUIT METHOD

This method gives a clearer marmalade. Again, you need to scrub the fruit to remove any wax or residue, then remove the hard 'star' from the top. Cut each fruit in half and squeeze out the juice into a large bowl. Set aside the juice and slice the peel and pith into thick, medium or thin shreds. Put the sliced peel into the bowl with the juice and add 2.5 litres of water. Cover the bowl with a cloth or film and leave the mixture to infuse overnight.

Next day, pour the mixture into a preserving pan, bring to the boil and simmer for about two hours or until the peel is tender. Add the lemon juice, sugar and honey and heat gently until the sugar has dissolved. Then boil rapidly for about five minutes and test for setting point using a thermometer. Take the pan off the heat and leave for about ten minutes, gently stir in any scum, then jar and seal.

Fruit curd

Traditional lemon curd is made using eggs, sugar, butter and lemons. Here is Susan Carvell's recipe (see case study below), which is absolutely delicious – no wonder it is a best-seller.

SUSAN'S LEMON CURD

Home-made lemon curd is far superior to the mass-produced bright yellow gloop you buy in supermarkets. It is pale lemon in colour and has just the right balance between sharp and smooth and, of course, there are no preservatives or colourings, which is always a bonus. Use best butter and free range eggs, organic if possible.

>   2 large juicy lemons
>   4oz (115g) best unsalted butter
>   6oz (170g) caster sugar
>   4 free range eggs

Using a double saucepan and with the heat on its lowest setting, put the butter cut into cubes and the sugar into the pan. While this is melting, grate the lemons and add the zest to the pan. In a separate bowl beat the eggs and add the juice of the lemons. Give it a good whisk.

Now turn your attention to the melted butter and sugar mixture. Give it a good stir to ensure that all the sugar has dissolved. Using a balloon whisk, gradually add the egg and lemon juice mixture, whisking all the time.

Now here comes the laborious bit. You need to whisk this for about 20–25 minutes until it thickens. You will know when it's ready as the whisk will leave a 'trail' when dragged across the surface of the curd. *Do not* be tempted to speed up the process by increasing the heat, otherwise you will end up with lemon-flavoured scrambled egg.

Pour into sterilized jars and seal immediately. When completely cool, store in a refrigerator for up to two months. Once opened, use within five days.

Jellies

Jellies tend to fall into two categories, sweet and savoury. The sweet ones tend to take advantage of autumn fruits like blackberries, crab apples and elderberries and are used when and where you might have jam; savoury ones are really sweet jellies (usually with an apple base) that have herbs added to them to use as an accompaniment to savoury dishes.

The basic recipe is the same for all jellies: 2kg of unprepared fruit to about 900g granulated sugar. The vagueness of the sugar quantity will become clear as we progress. I shall give the recipe for a basic apple jelly but if you want to make, say, a blackberry, or rowan berry jelly, simply replace half the apples with your chosen fruit. For a herb jelly simply add the herbs to the apples as you cook them, saving a few chopped herbs to add to the jelly at the final stage when you remove it from the heat.

BASIC APPLE JELLY

2kg cooking apples, or a mixture of cooking apples and crab apples
Approximately 900g granulated sugar

Roughly chop the apples, but don't peel or core them. Put them in a pan, cover with 1.2 litres of water and bring to the boil. Cover the pan and simmer gently for about 45 minutes, until the apples are very soft and pulpy.

Tip the contents of the pan into a jelly bag and leave to drip overnight. Don't be tempted to squeeze the bag – the jelly will turn cloudy if you do.

Measure the strained juice: for every 600ml juice you will need 450g sugar. Put the juice in a preserving pan, bring to the boil and add the correct quantity of sugar. Stir until dissolved then increase the heat and boil rapidly, without stirring, until setting point is reached. Take the pan off the heat and gently remove any scum with a slotted spoon. Jar and seal.

Pectin stock

You can use any high-pectin fruit to make this stock; I have found that cooking apples and/or gooseberries are very suitable for the job.

You will need 1kg of fruit in total – if you use cooking apples, just chop them roughly but don't peel or core them. Put the fruit in a pan with 600ml water and bring it to simmering point; cook gently for about 45 minutes or until the fruit is soft. Strain it through a jelly bag.

You can keep the pectin stock in the fridge for up to four weeks. (It can be frozen but it will lose some of its potency.) Use 150–300ml of stock for every 1kg of low-pectin fruit, adding it to the pan before the sugar is added.

CASE STUDY – SUSAN CARVELL

Susan Carvell is a passionate woman. Her eyes light up and her whole countenance sparkles when you mention those three little words – home-made lemon curd. She adores making preserves and if you detect something of the language of love in this description you wouldn't be far wrong. As Susan herself says, you have to have a passion for what you do otherwise the result will be lacklustre and will not have that certain 'something' that sets it apart from the rest.

Susan decided right at the beginning that she would make only the best preserves and to do that she uses time-honoured, traditional methods and uses only the best ingredients, sourced locally, wherever possible. She admits that it is not always possible to use locally grown ingredients – try finding a lemon grove in Lancashire! – but she supports local businesses by buying from the farm shop about four miles away from where she lives. Traceability is important to Susan: she knows where her ingredients have come from.

She decided that come what may, she would not compromise on her philosophy of 'source locally, make traditionally and produce quality', even if she had to charge a premium for her product. It is a cliché, but it is true that you get what you pay for: 'My customers get the best, so I have to charge accordingly,' she says.

Susan's first experience of making preserves was at a friend's house – she helped her friend make some marmalade. 'She did this from scratch,' says Susan, 'not out of a tin, like my mum had done.' And she was hooked. Making marmalade became her 'me time' and she found that not only did she find a real sense of satisfaction at the end result, but she enjoyed the process of actually making it too.

She soon started making jams and curds as well as marmalade and before long got to the stage where she was making far more than she and her family could eat themselves. She decided to offer some of her preserves for sale at the gate. Before she started selling to the public, however, she did some research and found that she had to register her kitchen with the Environmental Health Office. She felt very nervous about this. 'But I needn't have worried,' she explains. 'The Environmental Health Officer was brilliant. He helped me all the way.' Her kitchen 'passed the test' and so did she, having gained the necessary Food Hygiene Certificate, so it was all systems go.

Gate sales flourished, word got around, and she soon found her preserves were in demand, especially lemon curd, which is still her best-seller (she has kindly given her recipe, above). She was approached by a local farm shop for some of her preserves. In addition, a serendipitous chat in her local tea shop opened the way for Susan to use her preserves in some of her own home-made cakes which she now supplies to the tea shop.

I asked her if she had found any difficulties in moving from 'direct' sales, straight to the public, to selling to another business. 'Not difficulties,' she says, 'but one thing I learned was to put everything on a proper business footing, right from the word go. Everybody knows where they stand then. And don't compromise your philosophy. They want your product because it's top quality, and you have a good reputation.'

By this she means that you should agree a price for your product at the outset, keep meticulous records, and never agree to 'sale or return'. In addition, never negotiate on quality because the price of your product appears to be too high, even if it means losing an outlet: it takes an age to build a reputation for quality, but only a very short time to lose it.

Susan has been tempted to expand her business but she is happy to stay as she is. She explained that if she increased the size of her enterprise she would have to employ people, have bigger premises and so on, which she doesn't want to do. I touched on the sometimes awkward question of income. 'I don't earn a full-time wage,' she says, 'but I don't work full-time. I make enough to be able to treat the family and myself to extras, some luxuries.'

I got the profound impression that Susan isn't in it for the money anyway. She does it 'for the fun and love of it' (her words, said with a smile on her face and a twinkle in her eye). As I said earlier, Susan is a passionate woman.

CHAPTER 9

MAKING CIDER AND MEAD

I don't think there is anything that says 'English summer' as much as a pint of cider. Sweet or dry, from the keg or the bottle, but cold with that tantalising condensation as the warm summer air hits the chill of the glass and its contents.

Well, what is cider, and is it just made out of apples? In this chapter I look not only at that refreshing glass of cider, but also at other varieties of drink of a similar nature, like mead, perry and braggot. Some drinks have been lost to time, others become unfashionable; cider, mead, perry and braggot have begun to reinvent themselves and create a new future.

THE HISTORY OF CIDER AND MEAD

The history of cider and mead can be traced back millennia. Apples appear in many ancient stories and religious texts and many of these stories promote the mythical and medicinal qualities of apples.

Stories about apples abound: the Greeks have their tale of Hercules; there is the biblical Adam and Eve; Norse sagas and myths promised eternal life merely by eating an apple. The Norse goddess Iduna remained young by eating an apple a day, and Cormac, the Celtic folklore hero, used apples and the magic tree to achieve legendary status. Apples have been associated with love, fertility, eternity, consummation and eternal youth, so it is no wonder that our love affair with the apple continues.

We know that the Egyptians grew apples around 1000 BC. We cannot be sure whether they ever made cider, but we know that they fermented grain to make beer. In most cultures cider making came before beer, probably because apples could be gathered straight from the hedgerow whereas grain has to be farmed. We know that the Romans were very fond of cider.

Monks were partial to it too: in medieval times monasteries and abbeys brewed their own cider all over Europe. Some variations due to the soil and apple content and the available peripherals would mean that the monks might include wheat, soft fruits or pears. Whenever there was a glut of goods there was probably no better way to preserve it than to turn it into alcohol.

After the Norman invasion we see an influx of apple varieties and, in turn, the growth of cider brewing and drinking. But it wasn't until the 16th and 17th centuries that we see apple orchards being planted specifically for the brewing industry.

After a period of unpopularity, cider is now on a revival, with sales growing year on year. Exotic combinations that are being classed as cider are now available, such as ciders of mixed fruit, pear, and elderflower. I was asked once what I did with my quince harvest. We mainly make jellies and cordials out of them, yet I was told that it was possible to make a perry cider too. It might be a good way to use this under-valued fruit.

MEAD, PERRY AND BRAGGOT

Mead or honey wine

Mead is one of those drinks that people have heard of but can't be too sure whether they have actually ever tried it. Mead has been around for a lot longer than cider and has crossed a number of cultures and distances on its journey. We know that mead was drunk in China in about 7000 BC, and that it was popular among the people of India, featuring prominently in their Vedic religious practices. In AD 60 a recipe was written down by a Roman, Columella, for the production of mead.

Mead features in the folklore and myths from the Urals to the Atlantic. It is mentioned in Beowulf and found in most European cultures. It was especially popular in northern Europe where grapes were not grown. Claude Levi-Strauss noted that the invention of mead is a marker of the passage 'from nature to culture'.

Perry

Perry is a similar drink to cider but made with pears. There is a marked difference between any old pears and perry pears, which are not of eating quality and taste. If you are considering making a pomagne, it might be best not to use perry pears, which can give a harsh result, but to use your surplus edible pears.

Perry is generally made in the three counties of Gloucestershire, Worcestershire and Herefordshire, although it has crossed the border into south Wales, too. You can also find a version of perry in Fance, particularly in Normandy and Anjou.

Braggot

Braggot, or ale mead, uses a combination of mead and grain to make a weak beer. In the 15th century and through to the 18th century the main body of the population couldn't afford to drink wine so they would drink braggot. As the local waters were generally contaminated with a variety of waterborne diseases, braggot would be the safest drink because of the fermentation process it had been through. The 17th-century drunkards in contemporary drawings or Restoration plays would have been swilling tankards of braggot rather than ale, which would have been too expensive, and too potent to drink while working. Pure mead was for wealthier people, and wine only for the very few.

CASE STUDY – HAWKY

I met Gordon Burton, or Hawky (a keen fan of Hawkwind) as he prefers to be known, at a talk I was giving on bee keeping. Long grey hair, the smell of patchouli oil, and diagonal glasses perched on the end of his nose, he reminded me of my youth and somewhat hippy days. Hawky is a kind, caring man with a real passion for his craft of making cider and mead: he is desperate to become a full-time brewer and desperate not to drink all his brew.

He was looking for a supplier of local honey when we met. It was Hawky who told me about braggot. Full of enthusiasm for his craft, he was delighted to describe to me the process of making cider.

MAKING CIDER

Gathering apples

To keep his costs down Hawky doesn't buy apples but collects up windfalls and picks any apples his friends and contacts don't want. This clears gardens of rotting apples but he is also getting the best apples for his cider. And he has made lots of new friends along the way. He has collected apples from one garden for more than 20 years now and it all started when he glanced over a hedge and saw a whole orchard of apples going to waste. He asked whether he could pick them, and the rest, as they say, is history.

His system is to have two wheelbarrows for collecting apples in. One wheelbarrow takes the bough apples and the other the windfalls. Apart from avoiding cross-contamination of stock, he is able to single out the good from the bad. The windfalls go off to my pigs: apples and acorns, pigs love both. So he is able to get the first stage of brewing under way for little or no cost. He always makes sure that he gives a generous amount of cider or mead to his friends by way of a thank you.

He showed me some of the different type of trees available for cropping. Then we returned to his micro brewery, which is really no more than a converted garage, kitted out with hot water and wipeable floors and walls. He took me through the process.

First, Hawky said, you have to give yourself an incentive – remind yourself just how satisfying, and crisp and clear your own cider tastes, to avoid being tempted to buy at the supermarket!

Selecting your apples

He makes sure that the fruit he uses is fully ripe and never too heavily bruised. Any muck or rot on the apple means that they are consigned to the pig-bin. He leaves the apples for a couple of weeks in a dry and cool place – the garage, garden shed, a barn perhaps.

Over the years he has collected a number of old chest freezers that their owners have had no use for and would otherwise have been thrown away. As containers for keeping fruit in they are ideal as they let little air in and keep the fruit safe and secure.

Preparing your apples

Once you have selected your apples, make sure they are washed thoroughly and that any insects are removed. This may involve cutting the fruits in half or quarters to check for grubs. Don't allow anything like this to remain: it's a contaminant that can react with the fermentation process and cause sickness. Also have a look at the top and bottom of the apple and check for slugs.

One easy way of removing unwanted creepy crawlies is to give your fruit a saline bath; this is especially useful when using hedgerow fruits. All the grubs and the like will work their way to the surface, where you can skim them off and get rid of them. Don't use too much salt, though, as it could affect the natural yeasts and fermentation process.

You don't want any soil on the apples, either, but if you work on Hawky's 'two wheelbarrow' system this won't be an issue.

Crushing the fruit

When it comes to crushing the fruit, Hawky likes to cut each apple up into halves or quarters, which allows for as much juice as possible to be extracted from the apple.

In the past he has used everything and anything to mash the apples, from a rolling pin, to a piece of wood, to a metal pole. They all worked, but they were incredibly hard work. Now that he makes lots of cider, he has invested in a crusher. They are not too expensive and do the job admirably as well as being easy to clean. The crusher is literally a hopper with blades that are turned manually, and being made of alloy they resist the acid in the juice.

Pressing

You should at this stage have a bulky pulp, as Hawky describes it, which needs to be pressed. He showed me his pride and joy – a brand new press, which cost him only £200. With it he can press 20 litres at a time. The press is essentially a racking system which uses pressure to extract the juice.

Testing the pH (potential of hydrogen)

The extracted juice should be tested for its pH to check its acidity. If it is too high (too alkaline) this will destroy the fermentation process. This can be done by using a small soil-testing pH meter. You should be aiming for 3.9–4.0. If the pH is too low or too high you can adjust it by adding a quantity of precipitated chalk or malic acid as appropriate.

Checking the sugar levels

In order to check the sugar level in the juice, you have to find out the specific gravity, or SG. To do this you need a hydrometer.

You need a reading of 1070: then you are in business, as this means that there is about 15% sugar, which will result in a total alcohol content of 8.5% at the end of the cider-making process. If you want a less potent cider, something with a kick like a mole rather than mule, then you need to lower the sugar level and increase the SG. For example, by lowering the sugar content to 10%, you will have an alcohol level of 6%. This is assuming that all the sugar is fermented. And that is a key issue.

If the SG level is less than 1040 you will find that there may not be sufficient alcohol to protect the product during storage. You can raise the gravity by adding sugar: about 70g of sugar would raise the gravity of the product by around 5%.

Fermentation

Hawky, with the enthusiasm of a ferret in a pantry, went on to explain the fermentation process. The juice needs to be poured into a sterilized fermenting vessel – he uses a food grade plastic container, but you can use wood, as long as it isn't too damaged, or a stainless steel one.

The initial fermentation can be vigorous, to say the least, so you need to cover the container with just a cloth – you don't want to restrict the process too much. Once it has calmed down, top it up with either more water or more juice. Now is the time to exclude the air by fitting an airlock to the container. You don't need to add anything else at this stage; the cider is on its way, as the natural yeasts in the apples turn the sugar into alcohol.

You can let nature take its course, but if you want to have more control over the fermentation process there is a way. You add a Campden tablet, or to give it its scientific name, sodium metabisulphate, which will kill off the natural yeasts and halt the fermentation process.

You now have a 'clean slate'; you can then add a controlled amount of wine yeast which will allow you to manage the gravity, strength, and length of the process. It may seem odd to kill off the natural yeast and then replace it with more yeast, but this way you are in control.

Time to wait

Hawky took me into an Aladdin's cave of sounds. In a darkened corner a variety of plops and gurgles could be heard as the fermenting ciders at different stages sang out to each other. All are kept at a steady 15°C. Each container has two dates on it: its 'conception' and 'birth' dates, as Hawky named them, which range from anything between ten days to ten weeks. Hawky let me taste a ten-day-old brew against a ten-week-old one and then a two-year-old one. Like wine they get better with age.

Racking and bottling

Hawky picked out a container which he said was 'done'. When the cider has finished its fermentation process the SG is checked; if it is below 1005 it's time to rack it. You do this by syphoning the cider into a clean container, carefully making sure that none of the sediment is transferred. Fill your new container to the top, fit a new airlock and leave it to clear.

Some ciders tend to be cloudy and full of bits, but don't be discouraged by this, as 'scrumpy' is a fine product. Leave your brew in a cool, dark area to settle further. If you find that more sediment forms, repeat the syphoning until you have a clear brew.

When you have reached a stage of racking that you are satisfied with you add one Campden tablet per gallon of liquid. The Campden tablet will stop the cider from spoiling.

Bottling

When you are happy that the product is ready, that it is clear, there is no sediment and it's not 'racing around', bottle it into whatever size you are happy with. Plastic bottles are fine, as they have a tendency to move with the contents. Glass requires you to keep altering the caps as the fizz expands.

MAKING MEAD

With a scuttle and a scurry Hawky went off again to find a selection of meads. Out came a number of glasses and samples were poured. The first one I tasted was the essence of cats' pee, but the last one was a ten-year-old beauty: smooth, clear, crisp, with the inevitable hint of honey. Like a fine wine coupled with an aged single malt, it was indeed the food of the gods. Before I felt the effects of the mead take hold too much I asked Hawky to explain the basic method

First take 5 litres of water – originally it would have been rainwater. Use spring water if you can, or failing that boiled water that has been allowed to cool. Don't use water straight from the tap because it's chlorinated and will affect your mead.

Then you need 1.5kg of honey, a teaspoon of acid blend (you can get this from a home brew shop or a chemist), a teaspoon of yeast nutrient and a packet of champagne yeast. And that's all you need – except time.

As Hawky whizzed through the method I realized that it was quite easy. If you are using a liquid yeast mix, make it in advance. Measure your water to fill your demijohn, usually about 3.3 litres. Then return the water to a stainless steel brewing pot. Bring this water to a good strong, rolling boil and gradually add all but a teaspoon of the honey, stirring all the time so that it dissolves and doesn't just sit in a lump at the bottom of the pot. Also make sure that it doesn't boil over. Next add the acid blend.

Take the pot off the heat, cover it with some clean foil and allow it to cool naturally to around 37°C. Take the teaspoon of honey that you have saved and mix it with the yeast nutrient and packet of champagne yeast. Put this honey/yeast mix in the pot and allow it to dissolve. Pour the contents of the pot into the demijohn and then add the bung and a fermentation lock.

Fermentation and racking

Place somewhere cool and dark. If within 24 hours your demijohn isn't bubbling rapidly and there isn't a foam starting to form, then your mead isn't mead, it's mud and you will have to start all over again. Check it daily.

If all goes well a thick sediment will build up on the bottom of the demijohn. When about 2–3cm of sediment has built up it will need racking. To prevent the sediment passing to your next vessel you will need to syphon the contents between each. As you start to syphon off the mix, ensure that you control the depth of the tube so that it doesn't suck up any sediment: if it does you will need to do it again once the sediment has settled.

When you have completed transferring the mead, top up the demijohn with fresh water. Sterilize a bung and plug the neck of the demijohn and don't forget to add a fermentation lock. As the fermentation process slows down your mead should be exposed to as little oxygen as possible and you should disturb the mead as little as possible.

Check your brew on a daily basis. If you find that a new level of sediment builds up, re-rack it. If the water level falls below the bung, top it up with fresh water. After a couple of weeks the bubbles may disappear; this means that the fermentation process is over. Don't be too impatient, though, as the whole process can take between two and six months.

Bottling

At this stage bottle your mead and let it age like a good whisky. It is advisable to use bottles with a clasp cap. The ones on Grolsch bottles are the best sort to use, as the contents tend to become somewhat active. You can use screw tops or white wine bottles with new, clean corks.

Variations on a theme

There are lots of varieties of mead, from all over the world: Finland, Ethiopia, South Africa, Poland, Russia – the list is endless. In Finland a sweet mead called Sima is a seasonal brew associated with May Day festivals. Ethiopian mead is known as *tej*. During the second fermentation period raisins are added to control the amount of sugars and they also act as an indicator for when the mead is ready, as the raisins rise to the top. In South Africa mead is known by the Xhosa people as *iQhilika*.

The taste of mead can be altered by using different types of honey which will give you slightly different flavours. I would advise starting off any mead-making exploits using a cheap honey from any supermarket. Make your mistakes with this, and then you can experiment with Mexican Yucatan, Ethiopian Highland, Tasmanian Leatherwood or Scottish Heather until you find your favourite.

You could also add cherries to your mead mix, or even apples, tea leaves or grain – the possibilities are endless.

SELLING YOUR BREW

As with all these activities, no doubt you will want to try and make some income from them. However, there are a few rules to adhere to before you can sell your mead, cider and perry. Selling alcohol, even if it is not for profit, can still encourage the wrath of Customs and Excise. Swaps are not necessarily a problem, but to sell, even to break even, would raise more than one eyebrow at HM Revenue and Customs.

If you decide to sell, you will need a licence as a distributor of alcohol. You will also need premises that are compliant with the Environmental Health Office – all this takes investment of time as well as money, of course.

The law pertaining to this particular chapter is probably the most stringent, but at least clear legislation is available to direct you (see details of where to get information at the end of the book).

If you decide to leave the bottles of cider for swaps at the bottom of your drive, they will probably go very quickly with no return. If you distribute from your front door, you will find that the local constabulary will pay a visit very quickly, so be warned!

PART 4
Crafts

Introduction

In the next three chapters we look at some crafts that you may not have considered trying your hand at in the past. We could have looked at no end of interesting crafts – a few that came to mind were paper making, book binding, smocking, leather work or stained glass, but we finally opted for making chicken coops, soap, and dyes. The beauty of these three is that they link to other topics already explored in the book so far.

If you keep chickens, then why not make your own, bespoke coop rather than an 'off the peg' one, many of which are quite expensive. If you have been tempted to keep goats or bees, some of the milk and honey that your livestock produce can be used in making luxurious soap, as can some of the herbs and flowers that you can grow after reading Part 2. Herbs and flowers can also be used as dyestuff – and if you have angora goats you can spin and dye their hair.

This interlinking is one reason for choosing these crafts – another, and seemingly contradictory, reason is that they, like all the other chapters, can stand alone: you don't need to know anything about, or have the desire to learn about, any of the others covered in the book in order to have a go at these. Even though you may only want to experiment with them for your own enjoyment, all of them, too, produce items that are either barter-worthy or sellable.

CHAPTER 10

BUILDING CHICKEN COOPS

When my father decided on 'strict economic measures', it meant that we were skint. So Dad decided to buy a few chickens, build the coop himself and allow the hens to scratch on the drive. He built a chicken coop with an open section and a door and a lifting lid so that we could collect the thousands of eggs we were to have. By the time he had made it and gone off to collect his 'herd' of hens my sister and brother had commandeered the coop and set sail as pirates, leaving me behind. When my father returned, he was initially angry with my older siblings, but then became enraged that according to my mother he had been sold young cockerels. He had been told that they were frisky, lively young hens. We never saw an egg that summer and he had to go to out and buy more hens.

My father's attempt to build a coop was fairly basic. Years later, I successfully built my own.

WHY BUILD YOUR OWN COOP?

You could, of course, just buy a coop, but by building your own you will save money and get a great deal of satisfaction from making a home for a well-loved hen. I costed out the materials against the price of a pre-made one; in general a DIY one will cost half as much. In addition, the pre-made ones don't usually arrive fully assembled. It's a bit like IKEA for hens. Certainly the pre-made ones do their job and look very nice once you have put them together, but building your own simple coop should require only simple, straightforward tools; it should take only a day to make and that's including lots of tea breaks.

In this chapter I won't be giving you detailed plans of how to make a coop, just offering a taster of what sort of coops are suitable, depending on how many hens you want to keep, and where you are able to keep them. If you are then inspired to try building your own, information including plans are available on the internet, and some colleges now provide courses on hen-house building – have a look in your local college prospectus.

TYPES OF COOPS

There are hundreds of different designs for hen houses ranging from little more than a square box to something that resembles a traveller caravan! Generally speaking, however, they fall into three types of housing – the ark, the upright house, and the pitched-roof house. What you decide to build will depend on how many hens you want to keep, what sort of house you feel capable of making, and how you want it to 'look'.

How many chickens will you have?

The most important consideration in my view is how many chickens your coop will have to house. The accepted rule of thumb is that you will need a minimum of 1 square foot per chicken – this is the space in the coop, not including the run – so a coop measuring 3 foot by 4 foot could house 12 hens (this works out at approximately 10 birds per square metre).

So if you want to keep four hens, theoretically you will need a coop measuring only 2 foot by 2 foot, which to my mind is ridiculous, as well as being pretty fiddly to make. I would advise the size of coop to be nearer 3 foot by 3 foot for four hens – certainly, if you are keeping larger breeds they will need more space.

Portable house or static house

The number of chickens will to some extent determine whether you can have a portable or static coop: the more hens, the larger the coop, and the more difficult it will be to move. I have seen quite large coops with wheels on two corners and 'handles' on the other two so that, in theory at least, two people could move it like a wheelbarrow. How easy this would be in practice would depend on how heavy the structure is in the first place, and how firm the ground is. Even slightly soft ground would make moving something like that quite difficult.

How good are you at woodwork?

If your carpentry skills are not too bad, you will certainly be able to construct an ark or upright house, and probably able to tackle one with a pitched roof. To make your own coop you need wood – what sort should you use?

UNSUITABLE WOOD

Don't use wood that has been pressure treated with preservatives – this is potentially harmful to your chucks. I say 'potentially' because some manufacturers say that the preservatives are not harmful, but it's best to err on the side of caution.

Don't bother with stuff like MDF either – once moisture gets in it will soon buckle.

SUITABLE WOOD

One of the best timbers to use is softwood like pine or fir, which you then paint with a pet-friendly sealer or paint suitable for external use. (It will say on the tin whether it is suitable for pet houses; I have found that substances labelled as 'eco-friendly' are good to use.)

Alternatively you can use hardwood which is rot-resistant, like cedar or tropical hardwoods. The main minus point about this sort of wood is the cost.

SUSTAINABLY SOURCED WOOD

Whatever timber you use, make sure that it is sustainably sourced. There is little point in trying to live the local 'good life' if you are adding to global environmental problems by buying illegally logged timber. Look for wood that has the Forest Stewardship Council (or similar certifying body) stamp on it, which means that the timber comes from reputable, well-managed sources.

RECLAIMED WOOD

Reclaimed wood is certainly a good environmental choice. Be aware, though, that it might have been treated with preservative, and older wood might have been doused in creosote, which you should avoid at all costs. From 30 June 2003 it has been illegal to use creosote as a wood preservative, so unless you know that the reclaimed timber is younger than that, you should steer clear.

TOOLS

Do you already have the right tools for the job? If you have to buy a whole new set of tools just to make one small coop, it may not be economically viable, unless you know that you will use them again.

BE REALISTIC

Be realistic about what you can achieve – there is nothing more frustrating than starting a project only to discover that you have to hand it over to your smug friend who has stood watching you struggle, then steps in and fits it all together neatly like a Lego pirate ship.

What do you want your coop to look like?

If your coop is in full view from your house then the chances are you that will want something more aesthetically pleasing than if it were tucked behind the garage, out of sight. Decide before you start what level of 'prettiness' you want so that it won't annoy you (or anyone else) every time you look out of the window.

WHAT DO YOU NEED IN YOUR COOP?

Nesting boxes

Whatever type of coop you build, nesting boxes for your hens to lay their eggs in are essential. As a general guideline you need one nesting box per four hens, and each box should be about 1 foot square – larger if you have a bigger breed of hen. Line the boxes with straw to make them comfy.

Roosts

Perching facilities for the hens to roost on at night are also needed. This can be something like a rod running the length of the coop, or even a cut-off ladder fastened to the wall at an angle. Each hen will need about 6–10 inches of roosting space, and the roosts should be at least 2 feet off the ground, so be sure to factor this in before you start making your coop.

Ventilation

Make sure that your coop has sufficient ventilation: fumes from the hens' droppings and carbon dioxide from their own breathing will soon build up if there is no means of it escaping.

DESIGNING THE CHICKEN RUN

How big should your chicken run be?

Before we look at the different sorts of coops you can make, let's consider the run. If you are going to keep chickens, you cannot keep them inside all the time. Hens need fresh air and to be able to scratch about outside – they should be allowed 'chicken rights'.

There is no set rule, but for four hens you need a minimum area of 4 foot by 5 foot (that works out at just 27 square inches each) but if you can allow an area of 3 foot square per hen (6 foot square for four hens) that is better. And allowing them the freedom of the garden – without ruining your prize veg patch or pooing all over your patio – that's chicken heaven.

The size of the framework you build for the run will be determined by the number of hens you have, and the shape of it will depend on the sort of coop you decide to make. The covering will be the same in each case, though – you've guessed it: chicken wire! It's easy to get hold of – DIY shops and even garden centres seem to stock it nowadays, although it will probably be cheaper at a farm supply store. Securing it to the frame is easy, too. All you need are some U-pins and a hammer, or a heavy-duty staple gun. You must secure the run after you have set it up to prevent uninvited guests (particularly foxes) gaining entry.

Things to put in the run

Hens are naturally woodland creatures, so try to replicate some of the features they would find in the wild. For example, provide shelter from the sun by screening part of the run with some canvas attached to the chicken wire, or even (I have actually seen this) fix open umbrellas in the ground – large golf ones without curved handles are ideal for this.

Give your hens things to climb up on to, such as a pile of logs or a series of upturned boxes. And they will love something similar to leaf litter to scratch around in –straw or bark chipping is perfect.

Hens are pretty intelligent creatures and will soon become bored if they have nothing to stimulate them, and this can lead to them picking on each other, particularly the weakest member of their 'clan'.

Portable runs

A portable coop will need a portable run to go with it. This way you can let the hens have a new area of grass to scratch about on when the current one is showing signs of wear and tear. The 'old' patch will soon recover because it will have been well fertilized by the chicken droppings. A portable run should have an aperture in the top to allow you access when it comes to placing fresh water and feed in.

THE CHICKEN ARK

The chicken ark is one of the easiest types of coop; it can be built in a day by anyone with just limited carpentry skills. The ark is a triangular-shaped construction with an integral run and is ideal if you are just starting out on your chicken-keeping career.

It's suitable for about three hens, but don't include a cockerel in an area this small: the hens will have no peace and nowhere to hide, and he will become very frustrated.

The nice thing about an ark this size is that it is portable – you can move it easily from site to site, every day if you want to. This is a great benefit as your hens will ruin the grass they are on very quickly so moving the ark regularly will avoid big patches of bare earth. It also gives the chickens a regular supply of fresh greenstuff, especially if the grass is full of weeds, which chickens adore and most gardeners don't.

The portable ark offers the hens protection from the sun, next door's children kicking a ball over the fence, hawks and foxes. But remember that unless a coop is secured to the ground, someone or something will get underneath, often a stoat or weasel.

The ark is also very easy to clean, especially if you have a high-powered jet washer.

Having a portable chicken ark can provide a good starting point for children to get involved with the responsibility of keeping animals other than the usual cat or dog. Chickens are surprisingly soft and cuddly and love to be petted. One job that you can easily delegate to children is the collection of eggs. Another one is helping with the mucking out – so that they realize that keeping animals entails a fair amount of dirty work.

THE UPRIGHT HEN HOUSE WITH RUN

The upright hen house is a better option if you want to keep five or six chickens, and possibly a cockerel. An upright house is static but has a portable run, which means that you can move the run around on three sides, as long as the house has a pop hole (entrance for the chickens) on each of the three sides, which can be closed or left open as appropriate.

Nesting boxes

Within the upright hen house type there are 'sub' categories, so to speak: those where the nesting boxes are inside the house, and those where the nest boxes extend to the outside and have their own roofs which can be opened to retrieve the eggs. I would always go for external nesting boxes, for the convenience when it comes to collecting the eggs, even if the construction is a little more involved. You need to put the nesting boxes on the side of the hen house that will not have the run attached.

Cleanliness

When you are choosing a design for your upright house you should make sure that it will be easy to clean. You must be able to access even the most distant corner of the house, otherwise nasty bugs will take up residence. I came across a design for a smaller house with a hinged roof that can be securely bolted shut – a brilliant idea because there is plenty of room to reach into the house to clean. This wouldn't work with a larger coop, of course; my point is that it should be as easy as possible to maintain and keep your coop clean.

Raise it off the ground

A fixed upright coop needs to be raised off the floor. I would place a coop the height of a breeze block off the ground, if not two. This is mainly to prevent vermin, and especially rats, from nesting under the coop. Rats will appear wherever they think they can get a free meal, so try to make it as difficult as possible for them. Another reason is that your coop's wooden floor will soon rot if it is in constant contact with the ground.

Even better if you can get hold of some staddle stones: mushroom-shaped blocks of stone originally used to raise granaries off the ground – the 'cap' of the stone was shaped so that rats especially couldn't climb round them.

THE LARGE PITCHED-ROOF COOP

If you are really serious about hen keeping and are looking to have a large number of hens, certainly in domestic terms, then a pitched-roof coop might be for you. These can house from 20 to 100 birds, depending on their size. (It's important to note that if you have more than 50 birds you must register with DEFRA.)

Building your own hen house to accommodate this number of hens is going to be a big exercise, and you will undoubtedly need very good plans, pretty good carpentry skills – and some help.

Your house will be strong, sturdy and weatherproof, able to stand up against a storm. It will have a full-size door, and at least one window to allow in lots of natural light and to give ventilation. Remember that the birds will remain outside in hours of daylight and make their way to roost as the light diminishes. If they return at twilight to find a coop in complete darkness they won't enter it for fear of what's inside and will struggle to find their places on the perching poles.

The garden shed alternative

The majority of large pitched-roof coops look much like converted garden sheds in terms of design, which leads me to believe that this may be a good option in terms of building your own. A garden shed can easily be adapted to house chickens – pop holes can be cut and nesting boxes and perching facilities added. So think carefully about the alternatives before setting about building your own large coop from scratch.

Where to put your coop

You will not be able to move your hen house once it is in place, so choose carefully where you put it, and also its location in relation to where you live.

We used to keep several hundred birds a couple of miles away from where we live. I realized very soon that it was totally uneconomical to drive there and back twice a day to let the hens in and out of the coop. I became a bit lazy and occasionally missed a visit or two, making sure that there was enough food and water for the hens until I next went. One night I didn't lock them up properly, a fox struck and I lost a good number of my hens.

I felt very bad that I had not looked after my hens properly. I invested in an automatic door, which worked on solar power: when the sun came up the door opened, allowing the hens to go out, and vice versa. I didn't lose another bird to the fox.

MAKING CHICKEN COOPS TO SELL

As well as making your own chicken coop, if you have good carpentry skills you may consider making some to sell.

And instead of making a standard, run-of-the-mill coop, why not be inspired by Charlie's story in the case study below, and have a go at making something different? As I said earlier, hen houses come in all shapes and sizes – even looking like mini traveller caravans. Some of these are truly works of art and the price (up to £4,000) reflects the amount of work and skill that goes into making them. And some people will find real pleasure in the pure aesthetics of a decorative coop.

CASE STUDY – CHARLIE HORN

Imagine a mini-caravan chicken coop parked up in the corner of your orchard, complete with painted exterior and steps to the door. A friend told me about an old chap called Charlie Horn (who's dead now), who made the chicken coop into an art form.

Charlie's working life was spent as a shepherd on the South Downs. He didn't have his own flock but was employed by the local 'farmer-cum-squire'. In those days (a good 80 or so years ago) the communities in rural parts of the country operated under what we would call the 'squire-archy', where the local landowner was the main employer in the village and also the main landlord, since most properties would be tied. Charlie lived in one such cottage and was entirely dependent on his employer for his livelihood.

Charlie would also make and maintain the hazel hurdles that were used as sheep pens. As a young man he would have liked nothing more than to be apprenticed to and learn the trade of a master carpenter, but such lofty aspirations were way out of his league. But he would potter about doing a bit of woodwork on his day off and in the evenings during the summer.

Among the things he made were pheasant pens and chicken coops. On one occasion his imagination got the better of him and he fashioned a chicken coop in the shape of a mini-shepherd's hut, complete with wheels and corrugated iron roof. His neighbours laughed at it, but the squire loved it – or rather his ten-year-old daughter did. So the squire bought it to put in the orchard for his daughter's bantams.

People in the squire's 'circle' saw and admired the novelty chicken coop, and Charlie was inundated with requests to make more. At first he sold them at roughly cost price, and charged very little for his labour. Charlie was no businessman and eventually the squire intervened and helped Charlie to charge a fair and proper price.

His coops were beautifully crafted: they had a stable-type door you could either open up fully, or in bad weather use the pop hole cut into the bottom half; there were steps for the hens to climb up and down; and because the coops were on wheels, they could be easily moved.

Gradually word spread and people all over the county were interested in Charlie's coops. He spent more and more time building his coops, and made more money out of them than he was being paid as a shepherd. To avoid difficulties with Charlie's tied house, the squire decided to employ Charlie as a 'shepherd's hut coop-maker' instead of a shepherd.

So Charlie realized his dream of becoming a carpenter of sorts, and both he and the squire made some money. Charlie was making coops until he died, and I wouldn't mind betting that in the corner of an orchard in Sussex somewhere you will still find at least the shell of one of his coops, if not the entire thing.

CHAPTER 11

MAKING SOAP

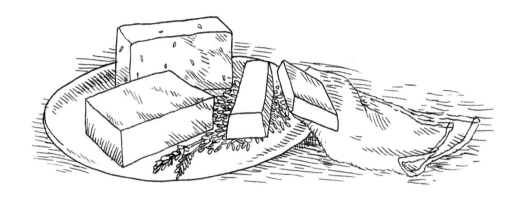

I have a feeling that soap is very much like many other products – once you have used a handmade, natural version you are unlikely to buy a commercially produced one again. This is certainly the case for me, and also my friends who have used the fragrant, creamy, cold-processed bars that I have given them as presents. They appreciate the fact that not only are they handmade (by Linda Clough, not me – mine are not good enough even to give away!), they contain only natural ingredients.

THE INGREDIENTS OF SOAP

I am not saying that commercially made soaps are bad. Economics and processing procedures, however, dictate that some ingredients are more suited to commercial methods of production than others. An 'up-market' bar of soap I was given as a present contained 17 ingredients: sodium palmate, sodium palm kernelate, aqua, glycerine, parfum, titanium dioxide, sodium chloride, tetrasodium edta, triclocarban, butyrospermum parkh, tetrasodium etidronate, butylated hydroxytoluene, citronellol, dipentene, linalool, and yellow and red colourings.

I recognized some of these ingredients immediately, such as aqua, parfum, glycerin, and sodium chloride. I looked up a few of the others I had no idea about and found that sodium palmate is a sodium salt of the acids derived from palm oil; butyrospermum parkh is simply shea butter; butylated hydroxytoluene is a fat-soluble compound that is used as an antioxidant; tetrasodium edta (ethylenediaminetetraacetic acid) is a chelating agent, used to decrease the reactivity of metal ions; and triclocarban is an antibacterial agent.

A number of the ingredients seem to be present to extend the shelf-life of the product or to make it 'safer' to use. Because these ingredients are present in the product, it must mean that they are harmless, but it raises the question, do I really want to apply some of these substances to my skin if I don't actually need to?

My favourite soap from Linda Clough (see the case study below) contains six ingredients: aqua, sodium olivate, sodium palmate, sodium cocoate, carum petroelinum, and honey. These are water; sodium salts of the acids derived from, respectively, olive oil, palm oil, and cocoa butter; parsley; and Lancashire honey. You get the gist of what I am saying.

THE SCIENCE OF SOAP

Let's have a look at the science of soap to understand what's going on when we make and use soap.

Chemical reactions

Making soap involves chemistry. Science was never my strong point at school, and some people immediately raise their guard if you mention anything to do with science, and especially chemistry. But chemical reactions are all around us: making and baking a cake involves myriad chemical reactions, as does starting and driving your car. Making soap may not be an everyday occurrence but the chemistry involved is no more scary than many other processes, although care must be taken when handling the ingredients.

Soap is produced after saponification has taken place. Saponification is the term used for the chemical reaction that occurs when an acid (in the form of oil or fat) is mixed with an alkali, otherwise known as a lye (usually in the form of sodium hydroxide, which is the 'proper' name for caustic soda). During saponification the alkalinity of the lye is all but cancelled out by the acid of the oil – the resulting soap is still slightly alkali but after a period of 'curing' the soap is more or less pH neutral.

What makes soaps go rancid?

Soaps can become rancid when the oil and/or fat content starts to decompose as a result of oxidation. Unsaturated oils and fats (like olive oil) are more likely to go rancid than saturated ones (like coconut oil and palm oil) but eventually all natural soaps will 'go off'. The time it takes for a soap to go rancid very much depends on the type of oil or fat you have used, and also on whether you have used a natural antioxidant, like grapefruit seed extract, which slows down, but can never prevent, the process.

How does soap clean?

In a nutshell, soap acts as both a wetting agent and dirt-holding agent. Soap molecules have 'heads' which attract water and 'tails' which attract dirt. When you mix soap with water the molecule 'tails' try to get away from the water, pushing up through the meniscus (the taut surface of the water) and dislodging and collecting dirt on the way, while the 'heads' are in their element sub-merged in the water. The dirt is held in suspension by the soap until it is rinsed away.

SOME DIFFERENT KINDS OF HANDMADE SOAP

Liquid soap

Liquid soap is really useful to have, especially in the kitchen and next to the wash basin. It goes through the process of saponification like a 'solid' soap, but the main difference is that a different kind of lye is used – potassium hydroxide. A recipe for a simple liquid soap is given later in this chapter.

Melt and pour soap

Many people begin their soap-making adventure with what is known as 'melt and pour' soap. This is where you use a ready-made soap base to which you add your own 'extras' in the form of fragrance and/or 'dry' ingredients, such as herbs or oatmeal. This type of soap doesn't need any 'curing' time, so you can use it as soon as it is cold.

Making this type of soap is a good way of involving children. The ten-year-old daughter of a friend had a 'soap-making' day for her birthday party (under adult supervision, of course), which was a great hit, especially as her guests could take their own bar of soap home with them – much nicer than the usual 'party bag' gifts. Again, you can find a recipe for 'melt and pour' soap later in this chapter.

COLD PROCESSED SOAP

This is the method usually used when making soaps at home, and although it is called 'cold' process it does involve using some heat. It also involves using sodium hydroxide, otherwise known as caustic soda, which calls for great care and the wearing of protective gloves and goggles. Cold processing produces a long-lasting soap with a soft, creamy lather, so it is well worth the effort and time it takes to make it.

This type of soap has to be left to 'cure'. When it has just been made it is still caustic; it has to be allowed to 'cure' for at least four weeks so that all traces of causticity disappear. There is a recipe for 'no frills' cold processed soap later in the chapter. First, let's look at the basic ingredients that are needed for this type of soap.

Ingredients

SODIUM HYDROXIDE

Sodium hydroxide (or caustic soda) is the common chemical base used in the cold pressed method. It is a combination of one sodium ion and one hydroxide ion, which in turn is made up of one oxygen atom and hydrogen atom. It is the hydroxide ion that reacts with the acid in the fat ingredient to make soap (which is why you can use potassium hydroxide to make liquid soap). That's enough chemistry!

The amount of sodium hydroxide you need depends entirely on the sort of oil or fat you are using. Each type of oil or fat has its own saponification value and these are used to calculate how much sodium hydroxide you need; for example, for palm oil this figure is 0.141 – so if you have 200g of palm oil you simply multiply that figure by 0.141 to get 28.2g of sodium hydroxide. If you have a combination of oils and fats, you need to work out each amount separately and then add it together. Details of different saponification values are readily available on the internet (see the information at the end of the book).

A word of warning. I cannot emphasize too strongly that you must take great care when using sodium hydroxide. It is highly corrosive in both dry and liquid form so you must always wear a long-sleeved garment (preferably something like a laboratory overcoat), latex or rubber gloves and goggles when handling it. Never become blasé about using this chemical; even a minor misjudgement can prove injurious.

OILS AND FATS

Oils and fats fall into two distinct categories: animal and vegetable. Animal fats are things like beef tallow, lard and butterfat; vegetable fats include palm oil, coconut oil and olive oil. If you are trying to be totally self-sufficient and rear your own goats, say, you could use the fat or tallow from the carcass to make soap. Vegetarians will want to use only vegetable fats and oil. It may be easier to get hold of vegetable fats than animal fats (unless you use something like lard which is readily available), although vegetable oils tend to be more expensive than animal fats. These may all be factors in your decision about which to use.

However, nearly all the recipes I have found for home-made soap use vegetable fats and oil, and personally I am inclined towards these too: I would much rather use something plant-based than animal-based on my skin. The most commonly oils used in natural soap making are olive oil, palm oil and coconut oil.

We all know olive oil, which is an unsaturated fat, liquid at room temperature. It is mild and gentle on the skin and so is ideal to use in soap. Many of us will recall Castile soap, originally made in the area of Castile in Spain: this soap was initially made with 100% olive oil – and was very expensive.

Palm oil is a saturated fat and is solid at room temperature. It is derived from the oil palm tree which grows in tropical areas. You might be concerned about using palm oil because of the environmental and ethical issues surrounding its production; ethically produced palm oil is available but you will probably have to search for it. Palm oil makes a hard soap with a stable lather, which is why it is nearly always used as an ingredient.

Like palm oil, coconut oil (or coconut butter as it is sometimes called) is a saturated fat which is solid at room temperature. It is used a great deal in the food industry, but it is also found in skin and hair products. It produces a firm soap with a lovely lather, but too much coconut oil can have a drying effect on the skin, so be careful not to have too high a proportion in your soap.

Other vegetable oils and fats, all with different qualities, can be used in soap making: avocado oil, castor oil, safflower oil, cocoa butter, and shea butter, for example. Recipes using some of these different oils and fats are readily available on the internet.

FRAGRANCE

Fragrance can be added to your soaps in the form of essential oils or fragrance oils. There is a difference between the two: essential oils are liquid oils that have been extracted from plants, whereas fragrance oils are generally synthetically produced. Again, the choice is yours.

Although it is not necessary to include fragrance in your soap, it sometimes adds a certain luxuriousness to get a hint of vanilla or ylang ylang. My favourite is lavender, which always reminds me of warm summer days pottering in my garden with the gentle hum of my bees in the background – so relaxing!

COLOURS

As well as fragrance you can add colour. Synthetic colourings are readily available but if all my other ingredients are natural, I am not sure I would want to add something synthetic.

Natural colouring can be obtained from ground spices such as cinnamon, cloves or turmeric, which give lovely earthy tones. You could also use any number of colouring obtained from dye plants, such as woad or weld (see Chapter 12 for more information). None will give a strong, bright colour, nor may they produce the colour you thought they would, because of the chemical reactions taking place, but it is worth experimenting.

PRESERVATIVES

If you are making soaps just for yourself or your friends the chances are they will be in small batches and used up very quickly, so there will be no need to add any sort of preservative to them. The only reason for adding them is to extend the 'shelf-life', prolonging the point when the soap will start to deteriorate. Natural soap makers who sell their soaps to the public might consider adding a preservative in the form of grapefruit seed extract (a natural antioxidant, it has antibacterial properties) but the majority do not. Again, the choice is yours.

'EXTRAS'

As well as colouring and fragrance you could add other ingredients to your soaps. Coconut and oatmeal, for example, provide exfoliating elements – but don't combine them in the same soap; less is more in this case. Honey adds a luxuriant feel – even better if it is from your own bees! And if you have been persuaded to keep your own goats after reading Chapter 2, you can use their milk in your soap, although this is perhaps for the more advanced soap maker.

Herbs and flowers which you can grow yourself can create an added interest. Herbs should be finely chopped before you add them, and some keep their colour better than others – parsley seems to be a good choice. Some petals also make a good addition: calendula (pot marigold) petals hold their colour well and add a beautiful yellow fleck to the soap. Small flowers, like individual lavender flowers, can be added too, but some seem to discolour during the saponification process, so experiment a little until you find something with which you are happy.

Equipment

Rather than give a list of equipment here I have included it in each of the recipes. The amount of equipment you need is not huge, although some of it must be of a particular type, which I will point out as we go through. The important thing to remember is to have everything to hand before you start.

SOAP RECIPES

You will notice that in all the recipes the amounts of ingredients are very precise. It is important to be exact in your measuring otherwise the recipe will not work.

Liquid soap

This recipe is for a simple liquid soap to which you can add some drops of essential oil at the end of the process if you want to make it smell even nicer.

EQUIPMENT

Gloves and goggles
Accurate scales
Heat-proof jug
Two thermometers
Stainless steel pan
Heavy-duty silicone or rubber spatula
Heat-proof bowl
Tea towel
Sieve
Soap dispenser

INGREDIENTS

29.5g potassium hydroxide flakes or pellets
Distilled water divided into three amounts: 72g, 70g, and 70g (212g in total)
110g coconut oil

METHOD

First of all put on your gloves and goggles. Pour the potassium hydroxide into the heat-proof jug and add 72g of water. It will react and heat up immediately.

Leave it to one side to cool down to 30–35°C – this is where you need the first thermometer.

Meanwhile, put the coconut oil and 70g of water into the stainless steel pan and heat it gently until the temperatures reaches 80–82°C – this is where the second thermometer comes in.

Take the pan off the heat and slowly pour in the potassium hydroxide solution, which should by now be at the correct temperature, stirring very gently as you do so.

Return the pan to the heat and bring the temperature back up to 80–82°C, stirring continuously. *On no account let the temperature go above 82°C or fall below 70°C.*

After about 15 minutes the mixture will become gel-like but will still be liquid. Before it gels completely, take it off the heat and pour it into your heat-proof bowl. Cover it with your tea towel and leave it to solidify for a minimum of 24 hours. (You can keep it in this state for up to eight weeks.)

Put the gel back into the pan and add the remaining 70g of water. Heat the two together but *don't stir* – this would cause it to lather up, which is what you don't want to happen. Instead, just press the gel into the water until they are amalgamated. You could add an essential oil at this point if you want to.

Take the pan off the heat and strain the liquid through the sieve into a jug and then pour into your soap dispenser. And there you have it!

Melt and pour soap

These are the easiest and quickest soaps to make.

EQUIPMENT

A large saucepan

A non-metallic, heat-proof bowl, large enough to 'sit' on the saucepan

A silicone or rubber spatula

A mould – a silicone loaf 'tin' is ideal (if you are using a cardboard or wooden mould you will have to line it carefully with baking parchment before you start: do not use metal)

INGREDIENTS

Ready-made soap base (available from soap-making stockists)

20 drops of essential oil of your choice

Any dry ingredients, such as oatmeal or lavender flowers

Colouring of your choice

METHOD

Fill the pan half-full with water and bring it to a simmer. Put the soap base into the heat-proof bowl and place it over the pan. Continue to heat the water, while stirring the soap base until it has melted.

Add any other ingredients and stir carefully. Pour the mixture into the mould and set it aside for a few hours until it is cold. Remove from the mould and cut into bars.

Cold pressed soap

Cold pressed soap is a lot more involved than the melt and pour kind, and timing and temperatures are crucial, so you need to know that you will not be disturbed.

EQUIPMENT

Gloves and goggles
Accurate scales
Heat-proof jug
Two thermometers
Two stainless steel pans
Heavy-duty silicone or rubber spatulas
A mould – a silicone loaf 'tin' is ideal (if you are using a cardboard or
  wooden mould you will have to line it carefully with baking parchment
  before you start: do not use metal)
A piece of card, big enough to cover the mould
A kitchen knife
A tray
A tea towel

INGREDIENTS

All ingredients should be accurately weighed – do not guess!

125g sodium hydroxide
340g cold water
454g olive oil
284g hard coconut oil
170g hard palm oil

METHOD

Make sure that all your ingredients and equipment are to hand and that you
are in a well-ventilated room.

Put on your goggles and gloves. Pour the sodium hydroxide into the heat-proof
jug containing the water and stir briskly with a spatula, being careful not to
splash anything. It will react immediately and start to give off fumes; do not

lean over the jug, and hold your breath if you can. The mixture will heat up; you need to put it to one side to cool down to 35–40°C.

Meanwhile, put the solid oils into one of the pans and heat them gently until they melt – do not allow the temperature to exceed 40°C. Now add them to the olive oil which you have put in the other stainless steel pan, ensuring that the temperature remains between 35°C and 40°C. Gently heat the oils if necessary but take them off the heat before you carry on.

When both the lye mixture and the oils are at the correct temperature, slowly and carefully pour the lye into the oils, stirring all the time. Do not whisk or beat the mixture because you don't want to incorporate any air, but you do need to stir it fairly vigorously to make sure the ingredients are thoroughly combined.

As you stir, the mixture will become thick, like custard. When it has reached the stage where a small amount of soap drizzled across the surface leaves a faint trace before sinking back into the mixture, it is ready to be poured into the mould. This stage can take 20 minutes or so.

Pour the soap into your chosen mould as quickly as possible once the 'trace' stage has been reached, but do not scrape the sides of the pan. Tap the mould lightly to settle the mixture, cover it with the card and place it in a warm, but well-ventilated, room.

Leave your soap for 24 to 48 hours until it hardens. Make sure that you are wearing gloves before you do the next stage because the soap is still caustic.

Take your soap out of the mould. If you have used a loaf 'tin' simply cut the soap into bars, pressing down firmly with your kitchen knife. This can be a bit like cutting a hard cheese so you may need to apply quite a bit of pressure to cut through cleanly.

Space your soaps carefully on the tray and cover them with the tea towel and put them in a warm, well-ventilated room. Now you must leave them alone for at least four weeks – six weeks is better – to let them 'cure'. During this time all trace of causticity will disappear and you will be left with a beautifully mild soap.

PACKAGING YOUR SOAPS

Once your soaps have cured, they are ready to be used, or given away as gifts. You can, of course, just pop them in a bag – paper, not plastic, because the soap has to 'breathe'.

You might cut a strip of pretty paper (handmade, even) and wrap it around the bar of soap, leaving both ends of the soap exposed. Add a label, telling the recipient what sort of soap it is.

You might wrap the whole bar in coloured tissue paper, or pop it into a small basket and tie it with ribbon – the possibilities are endless.

Linda Clough has her own distinct packaging – see below.

UNDERSTANDING THE RULES AND REGULATIONS

If you are making soaps for yourself you will not have to follow any formal rules or regulations – but as soon as you offer your product for sale to the public you must be aware of, and adhere to, any current legislation. Soap is covered by 'The Cosmetic Products (Safety) Regulations 2008' (available to download from www.legislation.gov.uk). If you want to make and sell your soaps on a commercial basis it is necessary to undergo training and an assessment – as Linda Clough has done.

CASE STUDY – LINDA CLOUGH

Linda Clough was concerned when she started reading the labels of various commercially produced soaps. Her daughter had eczema and Linda felt certain that some of the ingredients were exacerbating the situation. So she decided to make her own – that way she would know exactly what was in each bar and hopefully her daughter's skin would thank her for it. Being a trained aromatherapist, Linda already had a sound knowledge of natural products, so the decision to create her own soap out of natural ingredients was not a difficult one to make.

While visiting a number of country fairs in her area, she noticed that there were no stalls selling handmade soaps. This spurred her into action. Linda was serious about her new-found interest, so first she undertook training courses and assessments. When the time came she was able to sell her soaps to the public, rather than just produce them for herself or give away as presents.

Like other exponents of natural, handmade products, Linda is almost evangelical about her creations: she has stringent standards which she adheres to, and she is not willing to compromise on any front, even if it means she loses sales. 'I want to build an awareness of traditional, natural products,' she explains. 'My motivation is not to make money but to try to make people conscious of what they put on their skins.'

I know from first hand that Linda certainly doesn't overcharge for her soaps, bearing in mind the quality of the ingredients and the time and talent it takes to make them. This was one of her problems, she explained to me. When she first started selling her soaps she was almost apologetic about the price she was charging and felt that she had to justify the cost. Now she has learned to be confident and unabashed: her product is the best she can possibly make it and she is proud of that fact. The price has risen accordingly, but they are still a bargain!

Her customer base falls into two main categories: older people who are looking for a traditional product — the sort they remember from childhood; and younger people who are aware of environmental and ethical issues and are looking for a natural product.

She has a number of outlets for her soaps. She sells direct at country and craft fairs, where customers enjoy being able to speak to the person who actually makes the soap. And she supplies selected retail outlets, some on a sale-or-return basis, although her soaps are so popular that she rarely takes any back. Linda also has her own website (www.purasoaps.com), through which you can buy her soaps direct.

Linda keeps her packaging simple, allowing her soaps to 'breathe'. She promotes the 'handmade' aspect of her soaps, celebrating the fact that they are not a uniform size, and that each batch will be slightly different — this is what sets them apart from commercially made ones. Each bar is wrapped in a strip of handmade paper or brown paper and tied with ribbon or raffia, depending on the type of soap, and no two are ever exactly the same, which adds a dimension of exclusivity. She adds a label, detailing the information that she must, by law, give to her customers, such as ingredients, batch number and her business details.

Her soap-making enterprise currently runs alongside a full-time job, but she is focusing her mind to the possibility of expanding the soap business and reducing the amount of paid employment she does. She is also considering running workshops where like-minded people can learn the craft of soap making, but says that she ought to give a 'health warning' to anyone who is thinking about becoming involved: 'Soap-making can be addictive!'

CHAPTER 12

DYEING

The chances are that if you are reading this book you are interested in, and care about, the environment in which we live. I would guess, too, that you do your best to 'practise what you preach', perhaps by buying free-range eggs, supporting local businesses or recycling as much as possible. You may even have taken it a step further and been inspired to grow your own herbs, keep bees or goats, or make your own cheese – topics are covered elsewhere in this book.

One area that often falls outside the radar, though, is the use of chemicals. We can't get away from using chemicals – even natural products contain them – but we can perhaps be aware of using 'good' chemicals as opposed to those that may harm the environment.

One easy way of doing this is by using eco-friendly cleaning products. Another less obvious way is by being aware of what chemicals go into creating everyday items such as clothing and furnishings.

A friend of mine, Joan, has taken this on board in a serious way to the extent that she started buying items made from natural, unbleached, organic material as far as she could, and began dyeing them herself. I am not sure that I could ever be as committed as that, but I was intrigued when I saw the colours she created simply by using natural dyes. She still has to use some chemicals if a mordant is required (more on that later) or if she is using woad, but for the most part she uses naturally occurring ones.

Before the mid 19th century the only dyes available were those derived from natural substances, both plant and mineral, and sometimes animal. The craft of dyeing was so particular and required such knowledge that guilds of master dyers were formed as early as the 12th century. With the opening of sea and overland routes to various parts of the globe from the 15th century onwards, the colour spectrum available to dyers increased: cochineal insects, which give red, were imported from the Americas, and indigo arrived from the east. They were all still natural materials.

In 1856 the first successful synthetic dye – mauve – was discovered by William Perkin, and his breakthrough paved the way for the future of synthetic dyestuff. Natural dyes were, for the most part, sidelined, mainly because the cost of production was greater than that for synthetic dyes.

Nowadays there is a renewed interest in natural dyestuffs and although it is unlikely that they will ever be able to compete economically with synthetic ones, individuals and small groups of people are keeping alive the skills and knowledge – much like my friend Joan.

Having seen what she could achieve, I was fascinated enough to have a go myself, under her tutelage, and below is an account of my venture into dyeing with woad. I have also used my lesson in using dyer's chamomile flowers to illustrate other parts. First, though, we'll look at some of the different sorts of dyes and 'raw materials' that are needed.

DIFFERENT SORTS OF NATURAL DYES

There are basically three different sorts of natural dyes: substantive, vat, and adjective.

Substantive dyes are those that can be fixed without the aid of any other substance and are mostly found in bark, leaves and fruits of trees, like walnut.

Vat dyes are similar to substantive dyes in that they don't need a mordant, or fixative, but they do need other treatments to release the colouring substance in the plant material since it is insoluble in water. Woad and indigo fall into this category.

Adjective dyes require a mordant to fully fix the colour into the fibre. A large number of plants require a mordant, even some of the established dye plants such as dyer's greenweed (*Genista tinctoria*), or dyer's chamomile (*Anthemis tinctoria*). Often a different colour can be obtained, depending on the mordant that is used.

DECIDING ON THE RAW MATERIALS

Dyestuff

The most straightforward way of obtaining your dyestuff (the dyeing 'agent') is to buy it from a specialist supplier. These are usually extracts of natural dyes which have been processed and concentrated into powder, crystal or liquid. They dissolve in hot water and are then ready to use in the dye bath.

GROWING YOUR OWN

Alternatively, you can grow and harvest your own plant material and process it in to dyestuff. Colour can be extracted from almost any plant, but some will result in more pleasing colours than others. A word of caution: often quite a large number of flowers, leaves or roots are required to produce an adequate amount of dye, so bear this in mind if you are thinking about 'growing your own'.

The obvious herbs to grow for dyeing are those whose Latin species name is *tinctoria* or *tinctorium*, which means that it is used for dyeing or staining (from the Latin *tingere*, to colour). Among these are alkanet (*Alkanna tinctoria*), dyer's chamomile (*Anthemis tinctoria*), dyer's knotweed (*Polygonum tinctorium*), dyer's greenweed (*Genista tinctoria*), indigo (*Indigofera tinctoria*), madder (*Rubia tinctorium*), safflower (*Carthamus tinctorius*), and woad (*Isatis tinctoria*).

In addition there are dandelion, eucalyptus, goldenrod, lady's bedstraw, rose mallow, rhubarb, tansy, weld and yarrow. This is by no means an exhaustive list but it gives you an idea about how many useful dye plants there are. More information about each of these plants is given later in this chapter.

After you have harvested your plant material you can either use it fresh or dry it to use later. (If you do the latter, make sure that it is thoroughly dry and store it in paper bags rather than plastic or polythene.) There are no hard and fast rules about the amount of dyestuff you will need, but Joan tells me that the general rule of thumb is you should use the same weight of dyestuff as the weight of fibre you are dyeing. So if you want to dye 100g of fibre, then you will need 100g of dyestuff in the form of petals, leaves or whatever part of your plant is used. This was the ratio that we applied when we used dyer's chamomile flowers – 100g of flowers is an awful lot!

To extract the colour from the plant material you need to immerse it in water and heat it for about an hour. Again, there are no exact times: much depends on the plant material itself, but we allowed the dyer's chamomile to heat for just over the hour, about 70 minutes. Turn off the heat and allow the liquid to cool before you strain it. It is now ready to be used.

Mordant

Some dyes need a mordant to act as a link between the material and the dyestuff so that the dye becomes permanently 'fixed' to the material being dyed.

There are two categories of mordant: chemical and natural. The most common chemical mordants are aluminium, copper and ferrous (iron): they can all be bought in powder or crystal form from a dyestuff supplier. These are suitable for all fibres, both animal (such as wool) and plant (such as linen).

The most frequently used plant mordants are tannin, high concentrations of which can be found in the leaves of the stagshorn sumac (*Rhus typhina*), and oxalic acid which can be found in rhubarb leaves. Tannin is more suitable for plant fibres, and oxalic acid for animal fibres.

The final colour of your dye can vary depending on what mordant you use. For example an aluminium mordant will give you bright, clear colours, whereas an iron mordant will give a darker tone.

The most effective way to mordant your fabric or fibre is to carry out the process before you dye it. This means submerging your fabric in a mordant solution, usually with heat, and then letting it cool, still submerged, overnight. Then take the fabric out of the mordant 'bath' and rinse it thoroughly in cold water. The fabric can then be dried and stored until you wish to dye it. Don't forget to make a note of which mordant you used.

When Joan and I dyed some linen using dyer's chamomile, Joan had already prepared the fabric with an alum mordant, aluminium acetate.

You can combine the mordanting and dyeing process, 'skipping' a step, which can save on both time and energy. You simply mix the mordant solution and dye liquid together and then carry out the dyeing process. This doesn't work with everything, and Joan has had mixed results using this method. She prefers to mordant first, if the dye requires it, and then dye.

Fibres – what to dye

We usually assume that the only things we can dye are fibres and, indeed, these are the most common materials to undergo the process. You can also dye other natural materials, such as wood and shells. It is certainly worth experimenting with a few small items, such as mother-of-pearl buttons, dropped into your dye bath to see what the outcome is. We concentrate on fibres here, however, and natural fibres at that, which fall into two types: animal and plant.

ANIMAL FIBRES

The animal fibre that springs immediately to mind is wool. Don't forget that silk is an animal fibre, too, and these two – silk and wool – are probably the preferred animal fibres for dyeing. You could also use camel hair or wool from alpacas. And if having read Chapter 2 you are have been tempted to rear angora goats you could have your very own mohair to dye, spin and weave.

If you do have your own 'fibre-producing' animals you can dye the material before spinning it into yarn. You must make sure that the fibre is thoroughly clean before you start any sort of processing. This cleaning, or scouring, is vital to ensure that any dye is absorbed properly. You can buy a special scouring agent which is tailor-made for the job from specialist suppliers. Even if you buy ready-spun 'raw' yarns, it is as well to wash them meticulously to remove any trace of residue before you dye them.

PLANT FIBRES

The two most common plant fibres used by dyers are cotton and linen, although you could use jute, hemp or ramie (a little like flax, from which linen is obtained, but coarser). Usually plant fibres have already been spun into yarn or woven into fabric, before the dyer gets their hands on it. Either way, it is a good idea to wash them before you start to dye them.

THE EQUIPMENT YOU'LL NEED

There is some basic equipment you will need even as a beginner. The first two items are not strictly pieces of equipment, but they are nevertheless essential: a source of heat and a good supply of water. Joan uses the old pantry off her kitchen as her 'dyeing studio'. It has a large Belfast sink, and she has set up a portable electric ring there, rather than use her kitchen cooker, so as to keep her dyestuff well away from any food.

Even if you buy in your dyestuff you will also need the following.

At least one large, stainless steel pot with a lid
A pair of stainless steel tongs for stirring and lifting out the fibre from the pot
A pyrex measuring jug
Kitchen scales
A colander or sieve
A pair (or several pairs) of rubber gloves

If you plan to extract your own dye from plant material, the amount of equipment you need will increase, but really only in the number of pots, large and small, that you will use.

DIFFERENT METHODS OF DYEING

Cool dyeing

Cool dyeing is the most straightforward method, although it may not always be the most successful – some dyestuff needs heat to be properly 'activated'.

You simply take your fibre or fabric (mordanted if necessary) and soak it in water for up to two hours to make sure that all the material is thoroughly wetted. Then put the wet material into the pot containing the dyeing liquid (the dye bath), making sure that the material is completely submerged and that it has enough room to move around freely. You should leave it in the bath overnight and check the next day to see how much dye the material has taken up. If the colour is not as strong as you would like, leave it for longer – several days if required.

Hot dyeing

As with the cool dyeing method, your fibre or fabric has to be completely wet before you put it into the dye bath. For hot dyeing you need a metal pot, preferably made from stainless steel. Gradually bring the dye bath to simmering point, moving the fabric around gently from time to time, and heat for at least 30 minutes, and possibly up to an hour, depending on the depth of colour you require. Turn off the heat and allow the bath to cool to room temperature before you don your rubber gloves and remove the fabric.

This is the method that Joan and I used when we dyed our linen with dyer's chamomile. We simmered the fabric for just about an hour before letting it cool. When we lifted it out it was the most subtle but subdued 'daffodil' yellow – stunning. I have since used the fabric to make a cushion cover which has pride of place on the armchair in my study.

DYEING WITH WOAD

You can buy woad dye as a powder but Joan uses fresh leaves from her patch in the garden. She explained that she did try the 'urine' vat method but the family objected to having to pee in a bucket which was then allowed to 'mature' for a fortnight(!) before she used it for dyeing, so now she uses the 'hydrosulphite' vat method.

We took just over 250g fresh leaves, cut them into small pieces and put them in a pot. We then poured boiling water over the leaves so that they were just submerged and left it for about an hour – plenty of time for tea and chat!

We then strained the liquid through a sieve and squashed the leaves down so that we extracted as much of the liquid as possible. By now it was a brownish colour – not the blue I had expected.

When the liquid was 50°C we added some washing soda, little by little, until the liquid was a greeny-brown colour. Joan seemed to know just how much to add, which she put down to a good eye and experience.

I was then told to grab the whisk (the sort with a wheel and handle at the top) and whisk the liquid for all I was worth. Apparently this was to introduce as much air as possible so that the froth that was building up turned blue.

Once this was achieved, we heated the liquid so that the temperature once more reached 50°C. Joan then sprinkled three teaspoons of sodium hydrosulphite over the surface to remove the oxygen, which seemed somewhat perverse, after all the effort I had used getting air into it. We took the pot off the heat and allowed it to cool for about 45 minutes.

Now we could start dyeing my fabric. I carefully lowered it into the pot of dye, making sure that it was totally submerged. I wanted quite a 'rich' colour, so Joan suggested we leave it for about 20 minutes. Meanwhile Joan filled a bowl with cold water.

After 20 minutes I lifted the fabric out of the dye and Joan told me to immerse it in the bowl of cold water and then to lift it out. Apparently this helps to reduce any 'blotching' of colour.

As soon as the fabric was exposed to the air it started to turn blue – true alchemy to my mind. We pegged the fabric to a line strung above the sink and left it to allow the colour to develop. After about 15 minutes it was just the shade I wanted so I rinsed it two or three times in clear water then washed it and rinsed it again and hung it up to dry.

I cannot begin to tell you what a thrill it was to see my piece of cotton turn a beautiful shade of blue before my very eyes. If only chemistry lessons at school had been this exciting!

DYE PLANTS YOU CAN GROW YOURSELF

ALKANET
Alkanet or dyer's bugloss (*Alkanna tinctoria*) is a hardy perennial plant that does best in very well-drained, slightly alkaline soil. It can be successfully grown from seed but the seeds are notoriously difficult to get hold of. Nearly everyone purchases dyestuff from specialist suppliers.

No mordant is necessary to obtain a dull lavender colour, but if you use alum mordant you will get deeper purple and lavender colours. Use equal weights of dyestuff and fabric.

DANDELION
You may not want to encourage dandelions (*Taraxacum officinale*) in your garden since it can be found growing wild in every part of the country and can easily be harvested. If you decide to grow it, make sure you dead-head before it has a chance to set seed otherwise your herb garden will quickly be overrun by it.

It produces shades of yellow and green. A mordant is recommended. Use equal weights of dyestuff and fabric.

DYER'S CHAMOMILE

Dyer's chamomile (*Anthemis tinctoria*) is a hardy perennial plant which is historically extremely important as a dye plant. It self-seeds freely and tolerates most soils except where it is waterlogged.

It produces shades of yellow and green. A mordant is recommended. Use at least equal weights of dyestuff and fabric – use more dyestuff for a stronger colour.

DYER'S GREENWEED

Dyer's greenweed (*Genista tinctoria*) has been used since Roman times to produce yellow dye. It is a hardy, deciduous shrub which is best propagated by cuttings. It likes well-drained soil.

A mordant is recommended. Use equal weights of dyestuff and fabric.

DYER'S KNOTWEED

Dyer's knotweed (*Polygonum tinctorium*) is also known as Japanese indigo and its leaves do indeed produce shades of blue very similar to *Indigofera* species. It's a tender annual plant but is easily grown from seed. It needs a rich, fertile soil and full sun to flourish.

No mordant is needed to produce blues, but for shades of tan, use an alum mordant. Use three times the weight of dyestuff to fabric.

EUCALYPTUS

Eucalyptus grows well in our climate – some would say too well. It can reach massive proportions but if you prune it back periodically and use the foliage with cut flowers or as in this case as dyestuff then you can keep it well within bounds. The leaves are tough, so they need to be cut up into small pieces before processing.

Without a mordant you get a rusty orange colour but you can extend the range if you do use one. Use equal weights of dyestuff and fabric.

GOLDENROD

Goldenrod (*Solidago* sp.) is a hardy, herbaceous perennial which is extremely easy to grow from seed or is readily available to buy at nurseries and garden centres. It tolerates just about any soil.

It produces shades of yellow and green. A mordant is recommended. Use equal weights of dyestuff and fabric.

INDIGO

Indigo (*Indigofera tinctoria*) is a frost-hardy shrub and although it can be grown successfully in our climate, most dyers in the UK rely on woad or dyer's knotweed.

LADY'S BEDSTRAW

Lady's bedstraw (*Galium verum*) is a hardy perennial plant which is grown for its roots, which yield a red colouring similar to madder. It can be grown from seed, but you must leave the plants undisturbed for at least two years before you can harvest the roots. For this reason, it is worth buying some plants to begin with.

A mordant is recommended. Use four times the weight of dyestuff to fabric.

MADDER

Madder (*Rubia tinctorium*) is a hardy perennial plant which is easily grown from seed, but because it is the roots that produce the red pigment which dyers are after it is as well to buy some established plants so that you can begin to harvest sooner. The plant tops produce subtle shades of pink. Madder likes most fertile garden soils but would benefit from the addition of a little lime.

An alum mordant is recommended. Use equal weights of dyestuff and fabric.

ROSE MALLOW

This is the hardy hibiscus, which will grow quite happily in our climate. It is a deciduous shrub which can grow to two metres in height. Choose a variety with red or deep pink flowers – these will give you a lovely range of muted pink colours.

A mordant is recommended. Use equal weights of dyestuff and fabric.

RHUBARB

We all know rhubarb (*Rheum* sp.) from the stems we use in cooking, but it also makes a superb dye plant. You can grow it from seed but it is best bought as a 'crown' from a nursery or garden centre, where you can find ornamental as well as culinary varieties. It likes rich soil, so mulch it each year with some well-rotted manure.

A mordant is not needed to produce shades of yellow. If an alum mordant is used you will get a peachy/orange colour. Use equal weights of dyestuff and fabric.

SAFFLOWER

Safflower (*Carthamus tinctorius*) is a hardy annual so must be grown from seed each year. It can cope with most soils, but it must have a sunny position.

It produces lovely pinks and yellows. No mordant is required, but it will improve the quality of the yellow. Use equal weights of dyestuff and fabric.

TANSY

Tansy (*Tanacetum vulgare*) is a hardy perennial which is very easily grown from seed. Once established, it spreads rapidly unless it is kept in check. As well as being a good dye plant, a vase of tansy flowers in your kitchen will keep the flies at bay.

It produces shades of yellow. A mordant is recommended. Use equal weights of dyestuff and fabric.

WELD
Weld or dyer's rocket (*Reseda luteola*) is a hardy biennial, which means that it flowers in its second year of growth, so it is best to grow a new 'batch' of plants from seed each year. It is the plant tops, both flowers and stems, that are used. It is one of the oldest yellow dye plants, giving subtle hues and shades depending on whether or not a mordant is used.

A mordant is not needed to produce a creamy, pale yellow. A copper mordant gives a rich yellow with a green tinge. Use equal weights of dyestuff and fabric.

WOAD
Woad (*Isatis tinctoria*) is perhaps the best known of all the natural dye plants. It is a biennial but since it is the leaves that yield the dye it is best grown as an annual. This is unless you want to save your own seed, in which case you can let just one plant flower. The seed is best sown in situ, because it does not transplant happily. Being a vat dye it needs special treatment – one of the easiest methods is described above.

It produces blues and tans. No mordant is required. Use equal weights of dyestuff and fabric.

YARROW
Yarrow (*Achillea millefolium*) is a hardy perennial that prefers a free-draining soil. It can be grown from seed, or you can buy a huge variety of different cultivars from garden centres or nurseries, all of which will yield dye.

It produces subtle shades of yellow and green. A mordant is recommended. Use equal weights of dyestuff and fabric.

USING YOUR DYED MATERIAL

So far I have looked at the process of dyeing and some of the plants you can grow yourself, and there is much satisfaction to be gained from just doing this. But what can you do with the material that you have dyed? Yarn can be used to weave a fabric of your own, or to knit or crochet with. Fabric can be used to make small items of clothing or furnishings. Either way, it's fun to make things for yourself and your family and friends.

If you are considering making and selling some of your handiwork, because your product has undergone a specialist process – hand dyeing – you can charge a premium for it. This is true for knitting and crochet yarns as well as 'finished' items like cushion covers or scarves. Unlike foodstuffs, your product has no 'sell by' date, so you can dye and make things as and when you have time in order to sell them at optimum times during the year.

My friend Joan not only loves dyeing 'ready-made' items, she also loves knitting (apparently it's what she does to relax in the evenings – she has to sit down to do it!). Throughout the year she knits a whole range of scarves, from delicate, cobweb-like constructions to simple, chunky knits. These she stockpiles until December then takes them to her local Christmas craft fair. She labels each scarf so that customers know that they are hand-dyed and hand-knitted, and presents each one in a beautiful, tissue-lined box.

Each year she has about 40 to sell – an output of not quite one a week – and each year she sells them all. Prices range from £9.99 for the simplest pattern and cheapest yarn, to £49.99 for the most intricate design and costliest thread, which are particularly beautiful. Joan says that if she took into account the hours spent dyeing and knitting she is definitely running at a loss, but she does it for the love of it.

CASE STUDY – TERESINHA ROBERTS

Another person who does it for the love of it but has also built a successful business, is Teresinha Roberts.

Teresinha Roberts leads a highly colourful life. She is a qualified textile artist and while learning her craft she became interested in the dyeing process, being inspired particularly by the use of natural dyes. Some time later she found herself in Birmingham, with an allotment, and she glimpsed something different to grow in one of her herb seed catalogues: dye plants. The seed was set, quite literally, when she started growing, and using, her own dye plants, such as woad, madder and weld.

She and her husband set up a website to spread the word about natural dyes and before too long they were getting enquiries about whether they sold dye materials. And so her business was born.

Just three years after she made her first sale she gets on average 25,000 visitors a week to the website, which her husband maintains – not everyone buys, of course, but those who do often purchase dyes and mordants in kits. She only sells over the internet: 'Everything else is so time-consuming,' Teresinha says; not that she has any time to spare.

Her business has taken over her life and continues to grow. She has had enquiries from handmade paper producers in India and Nepal and she now sells their beautiful paper, dyed with her own natural dyes, as well as her own handmade, hand-dyed greetings cards, on her website, making her a truly international business.

Teresinha is also hoping to develop another strand – dyeing wool to sell, but this would need a bigger workshop than the one she currently has in the Custard Factory, a prestigious artists' complex in Birmingham. She would also like more space in order to be able to run workshops to enthuse other people with her passion for natural dyes. Like all our case study experts, Teresinha is an ardent exponent of her craft, and although she makes a living from it, she hasn't lost sight of her primary motivation.

Her business is thriving but it has been hard work and not without difficulties. She knew nothing about running a business before she started, and although there are helpful courses available through the likes of Business Link, she has more or less learned 'on the job'. 'But you shouldn't be afraid of making mistakes,' she says. 'You are more likely to graze your knee than break your leg!'

And where does she see herself in five years? 'My dream is to have a warehouse and a forklift truck,' she chuckles. And I have no doubt her dream will come true.

PART 5
Practicalities

CHAPTER 13

THINGS YOU NEED TO KNOW

If you intend to try putting some of the suggestions we have made in the previous chapters into practice, there are some things that you need to be aware of. Some of this is the 'nitty-gritty' stuff that we need to know about rather than want to know about – and some of it may not be relevant at all if you don't intend to sell any of your produce. But for those of you that do, it is worth spending a few minutes going over some of the areas that you will have to bear in mind.

SMALLHOLDING REGISTRATION

If you want to keep livestock you need to register your property as a smallholding. Contact DEFRA and you will be issued with a County Parish Holding (CPH) number. (It will look something like this: CPH 09/018/ 0085 09.)

Once you have this, contact your local Animal Health Department to let them know that you are intending to keep livestock and they will allocate you a herd or flock number. Only then can you bring livestock onto your land.

You will be sent lots of advice about the necessary procedures for moving your animals (including taking them to slaughter, if that is part of your agenda), and updates about new regulations from time to time. It sounds a bit daunting, but it is necessary for the welfare of your, and other people's, animals.

REVENUE AND CUSTOMS

Before we get carried away with ideas of untold riches coming from our new enterprise, it is as well to address an area which is unpleasant to most people – the Inland Revenue.

Exchange and bartering

The area of exchange and bartering is a little complicated. It seems to depend on whether or not you are a trade or business.

If you keep a few chickens and swap half a dozen eggs for a jar of your neighbour's jam then the Revenue isn't overly interested. If your business is producing eggs and you are regularly exchanging them for your week's supply of meat from the butcher, say, then apparently that is a different story.

It all seems to depend on whether the exchange or barter is a 'social favour' or a 'professional or trade exchange'. If you are in any doubt, seek advice either direct from Revenue and Customs or from an accountant or financial adviser.

Selling

The story is different if you are selling your produce for hard cash. My accountant is at pains to stress that however much or little anyone makes from selling any produce, goods or services, that income must be declared to the Revenue. As a consequence you must keep scrupulous financial records of the income and expenses connected to your enterprise, no matter how small. This means that you will be able to determine just how much profit you are making – and this is the bit the taxman is interested in.

I would strongly advise you to seek out an accountant to help you with this. My accountant not only deals with my tax affairs but also gives me sound financial advice, and his modest annual fee is worth every penny.

Registering for VAT

If your enterprise is growing into more than just a hobby you may consider registering for VAT. According to the HMRC website (www.hmrc.gov.uk) this is compulsory 'if your turnover of VAT taxable goods and services supplied within the UK for the previous 12 months is more than the current registration threshold of £70,000, or you expect it to go over that figure in the next 30 days alone'.

I suspect that not many of us will reach that sort of turnover very quickly, but if you sell zero-rated goods, such as food (for example honey, most culinary herbs, fruit), then it might be worth registering because you can claim back any VAT on your input purchases. Again, seek advice from your accountant.

TRADING STANDARDS, ENVIRONMENTAL HEALTH, AND FOOD HYGIENE

Before you offer any produce (even if it is not foodstuff) for sale to the public, whether via direct sales or through a third party, it is worth making some checks with any regulatory bodies and informing them of what you intend to do.

Trading Standards

Trading Standards is a local authority service which deals with things like weights and measures, animal welfare, food, labelling, and fair trading. Your local Trading Standards Office is very easy to find on the internet – you simply put your postcode in the search section on www.tradingstandards.gov.uk and up pops your local office. This website also has basic information covering topics like 'Before Buying Hens' and 'Food Labelling'. A lot more information is available from your local office: remember that they are to help you, not to try and catch you out.

Environmental Health

Again, this is a local authority service. If you are preparing and selling any sort of food items you need to contact this department as they will give you vital advice, and help you to understand any legislation that applies to what you are doing.

They can supply you with an application form for the 'Registration of a Food Business Establishment'. This is a form which you must fill in and submit 28 days before you intend to start preparing food for sale. Don't panic! It is very straightforward and helps them to assess whether you need to be approved or registered.

To get in touch with your local Environmental Health Officer, contact your local government office and they will give you the correct department. Alternatively, put 'Environmental Health' and your town in an internet search engine and a relevant website will come up.

Food hygiene

If you are handling food you will undoubtedly be advised to pass the 'Level 2 Award in Food Safety in Catering'. This is a nationally recognized qualification that is run at many further education colleges. The course usually lasts just one day and you take the exam at the end of it.

CHAPTER 14

SHARING AND SELLING YOUR PRODUCT

When you start raising livestock, growing things, or making things, the primary motivation for most people is to satisfy their own practical, aesthetic or holistic needs – and often both. There is a deep satisfaction to be gained from keeping bees purely for the joy of it, for example, but there is added fulfilment when you taste the first spoonful of honey made by your own bees. Once those personal needs are satisfied many people find that they have a surfeit of goods or produce and begin looking at ways to 'dispose' of them.

First we look at something that we think is of equal importance to selling, if not more so – exchanging and bartering. This is an especially useful way of getting rid of excess goodies when you don't wish to make use of them yourself but don't want to go down the selling route either.

201

Then we look at how to sell your products. Our case study experts who have made businesses out of their interests use various methods of selling their produce to the public and we suggest a few that you too could employ.

EXCHANGING AND BARTERING

In the previous chapter we touched on exchange and bartering, pointing out the difference between informal, 'social' exchange and running it as a 'business'. Either way, there has been a recent upsurge of exchange, swap and bartering schemes. Some are locally based, others are spread much wider using the internet. The principle is the same with all of them, and that is that no money changes hands. And there is the underlying supposition that someone will want what you have to offer, even if it isn't a 'straight swap'.

If your goats are producing more milk than you know what to do with why not try and swap it with a neighbour who might have a glut of plums, for example. It's a grand way of making the most of what you and your neighbours have to offer and when you get involved in this way or change of life, you will quickly realize you are not on your own.

My family had first-hand experience of this type of transaction. One year my sister's Christmas dinner was entirely home-grown or bartered. The Christmas pudding and cake were no problem – she made those. She also grew her own vegetables. But she was lacking a turkey, the sausages and bacon to go with it, and cream to go with the pudding.

She came to an agreement with the local farmer who reared free-range turkeys that she would bake a cake for him each month throughout the year in return for an oven-ready turkey at Christmas. The sausages and bacon came from the village butcher in exchange for a chocolate yule log, and the cream (and also some cheese) from the dairy in the next village cost her a dozen mince pies.

Everyone was happy and no money had changed hands. This was very much an ad hoc arrangement, but it could have been extended to include and benefit others.

Remember, though, that if you have a surplus of something that you want to offer for exchange, there is a chance that everyone else is in a similar position to you.

'SELLING' YOUR PRODUCT

Branding and packaging

It is worth giving some thought to your 'corporate image' when selling your product, even on a semi-professional basis. This sounds a little grand but you do need to find a 'brand' name, and, if you like the idea, a logo and colour scheme. This is particularly important if you are going to label your product, which nine times out of ten you will be required to do by law. It might also be worthwhile thinking about packaging, particularly with things like herbs and soaps.

You may not be aiming to compete with the 'big boys' but you do need a professional approach to your enterprise. You may opt to keep your image simple, emphasizing and celebrating the fact that your product is handmade and home-made. On the other hand you might decide on something highly sophisticated, giving the impression of total luxuriance and exclusivity. Whatever you decide, this is the name and image that you want people to remember, and to keep coming back for.

PRICING YOUR PRODUCT

Whatever you sell, whether it is a pot of jam, wedge of cheese or bar of soap, you have to decide how much you are going to charge for it. You could look around and see what other, similar, products are priced at and then pluck a comparable figure out of the air – but perhaps this isn't the best way to go about things!

What you really need to do first is work out how much it has actually cost you to get your product to the point where it can be sold – not just in terms of raw materials, but including labour costs and other overheads, like electricity and so on. Often people underestimate, or ignore entirely, the cost of their own labour because, they argue, if they did take it into account they would never make any money. This is something you will have to decide for yourself – although it's a different matter if you are employing someone, of course.

Getting to a 'cost' figure per item can be fairly complicated and time-consuming and you may find that you have to make educated guesses at some of the expenses, but your aim is to have at least a close idea.

Then you have to settle on what profit margin is reasonable: 15%, 25%, 75%, 150%? Add this to your cost figure and decide if this is reasonable in terms of what your customers would be willing to pay. You would be surprised how many people expect homemade and hand-made goods to be cheaper than shop-bought, but stand your ground – your product is special (sometimes unique if you have a 'secret recipe'), so the price should reflect that.

You need to be aware, however, of what other retailers are charging for a similar product. If you find that your final figure is unrealistic, you may have to reconsider your profit margin – up as well as down, if necessary!

As an exercise, I worked out recently how much it cost me to make a jar of marmalade. Costing the oranges and sugar was easy, as was assessing the cost of the jar, lid and label. What was trickier was working out how much electricity I had used, but I jotted down a meter reading at the beginning of the exercise and then again at the end. Of course, even this couldn't be that accurate because the fridge was running, lights were on, and my husband was working on the computer at the time: nevertheless, I could give a reasonable estimate of the amount I had used. Then I looked at our last electricity bill to see how much we were paying per unit and worked out a figure from that. I took my labour into account at basic wage.

The figure I came up with was that it had cost me £2.04 to make one jar. I decided to add 40% profit to give me £2.85. Was this reasonable? I thought so. However, if I added 75% profit, giving a selling price of £3.57, it would not be reasonable in my neck of the woods, although elsewhere it might have been. You get the idea.

SELLING YOUR PRODUCT

In effect there are two methods of selling your product – directly and indirectly. Direct sales are where the selling is done by you personally or by your representative, direct to the customer. I have in mind things like selling at the gate, or farmers' markets. Indirect selling is where you sell your goods to a retailer who then sells to the customer.

'At the gate' sales

This is by far the simplest way to sell any excess produce, and probably the one that best evokes a 'country' way of life. But you don't need a thatched country cottage with roses around the door to sell things at the gate – you can do it anywhere, as long as you have enough passing trade.

Make sure that whatever you are offering is already in a saleable unit: a jar of jam, a bunch of flowers, a punnet of raspberries, half a dozen eggs in a box, and so on. Don't have loose items which customers choose for themselves; pricing will be impossible.

You need to price items sensibly (to the nearest 50p, for example) and reasonably to attract passing trade. Set up an honesty box where customers can put the correct amount of money.

If you rely on an honesty box, though, be aware that although the vast majority of people are honest, not everyone is, and you may lose your entire takings as well as some of your produce. You have to decide if it's a risk worth taking.

As far as official advice is concerned about gate sales, the one area where there is anything specific is with eggs. The DEFRA website states that: 'producers with fewer than 50 birds are not required to be registered with an Animal Health Egg Marketing Inspector nor with the Great Britain Poultry Register'; and 'ungraded eggs sold direct to the final consumer at the producer's farm gate or sold by the producer locally door to door in the region of production will not have to be marked'. For more information go to the DEFRA website (www.defra.gov.uk).

Markets

Markets are another option. Investigate what opportunities there are in a certain radius from where you live, say 25 miles. You may find that there is a different market you can sell at every week, giving you ample opportunity to both buy and sell.

If you decide to sell at markets you need to get in touch with both your Environmental Health and Trading Standards officers. They will advise you about food safety, trades descriptions, labelling, weights and measures and the like. It can be quite involved, particularly if you are preparing food at home or selling meat or dairy produce, but don't be put off.

FARMER'S MARKETS

Trading at farmers' markets is a brilliant way of selling your produce and there are many benefits. You can often, but not always, get a higher price for your goods because you are selling direct; and you don't need complicated selling or marketing strategies. And the benefits are not entirely monetary: you get to know your customer and what they like; you can create an awareness about and offer information on your produce; you get satisfaction from knowing that your produce is appreciated.

Seek out your local market and talk to the stallholders about their experiences. Talk to the market manager about availability and prices of stalls; find out whether you have to provide your own table, and so on.

There can be certain rules and stipulations about selling at a farmers' market. For example, it is usually the case that you should have produced your goods within a locally defined area, often a 25-mile radius or thereabouts, of where the market is held. In addition you may need to offer 'tasters' if you are selling edibles like cheese or preserves. You will have to show the price of your goods, either on the individual items or on a prominent display. From the customer's point of view there is nothing more annoying than having to ask the price of things.

For more information about farmers' markets have a look at the National Farmers' Retail and Markets Association website (www.farma.org.uk).

Remember that your primary purpose is to sell your produce, so your stall – and you! – should be smart and welcoming. Make your stall as attractive as possible to entice customers – once you have two or three people looking at items it's amazing how often more are drawn in to see what is capturing their attention. And once you have an interested audience, it's a small step to get them to buy something. It is even worth taking time to do a 'mock up' of your stall at home beforehand to see where you can make improvements.

Decide what you are going to wear to promote a 'professional' feeling – you don't have to wear a white coat, but a clean apron is a good idea. That way people know that you are the person doing the selling and not another customer.

If you are handling food you may have to wear latex gloves; if you have long hair, tie it back. Make sure that your hands and nails are clean whatever you are selling.

You will also need product and public liability insurance, and if you have someone working for you there is employer's liability to consider too.

COUNTRY MARKETS

Country Markets Ltd is a cooperative enterprise covering England and Wales which deserves to be more widely known. It started out as part of the Women's Institute way back in 1919. In 1995 it separated from the main body of the WI to become WI Country Markets Ltd and then in 2004 the WI bit was dropped from the name altogether.

The organization offers individuals the opportunity to sell their home-made and home-grown produce locally, direct to the public. You have to become a member of the cooperative (it costs all of 5p – yes, five pence – to join) and adhere to some far from onerous rules. It's a wonderful way of not only selling your produce but of meeting like-minded producers and consumers.

There are about 400 markets dotted all over the country – for example, I found 11 in Kent, seven in Leicestershire, and three in Gwynedd, so you should be able to find one not too far from you. Have a look at their website for more information (www.country-markets.co.uk).

Fairs, fêtes and shows

It is often possible to book a stall at a local country fair, fête or show. These are ideal if what you are selling is a non-food product, like soaps, or has a long shelf-life, like preserves, so you can stockpile lots in advance of the big day.

The cost of hiring a stall or stand can vary enormously, from nothing to several hundred pounds, depending on the type of event. Sometimes the organizers will want a share in your takings, too, so you should weigh up carefully whether or not it is worth your while. It helps if you have willing volunteers to help you who won't want paying; if you have to hire assistance you must take that cost into account. Remember that the suggestions made above about presentation and appearance at markets hold true for other venues.

Internet/mail order

Another method of selling your produce is by mail order or over the internet. This lends itself more readily to non-perishable items, but some of our case study experts, such as Jekka McVicar of Jekka's Herb Farm, and Gill Pateman of Merlin Cheeses, use these methods to great advantage. There is the assumption, of course, that you have a website or catalogue through which customers can order. If you don't have either of these methods in place you would have to think carefully about whether it would be cost-effective to set either of them up.

Indirect selling

If you want to avoid direct sales altogether you can sell through a third party (wholesale). Some of our case study experts sell both direct and through a retailer, so there is scope to do both. Like any other method of selling there are pros and cons to selling wholesale, so again you have to decide what is best for you.

The main advantage of selling wholesale is that you don't have the worry of finding individual customers: it is the retailer's job to do the day-to-day selling, with all the problems that entails. The main disadvantage is that you have to sell to the retailer at wholesale prices. These will be substantially lower than the prices your goods will sell for in the shops because the retailer will add their margin to the wholesale price to cover their overhead costs and make a profit. It may be galling to see your jam for sale at £3.50 a jar when you know that you have only charged the retailer £1.50 – but that's the way it works.

You may also find that the retailer supports the idea of selling your product under their own label. I have seen this work to the advantage of both producer and retailer with regard to preserves: not only did the retailer pay more, albeit only a little, but they provided, and stuck on, their own labels, which was one less expense for the producer. Product information still has to be given on the label, however, so if you go down this route, check with your Trading Standards Officer first.

And finally . . .

There is no one 'perfect' way of selling your product: you will have to experiment and test the market. Do your 'homework' and find your 'niche'. And once you have, like our case study experts, you will never look back.

FURTHER READING

Bees
Cramp, D. (2008) *A Practical Manual of Beekeeping*. Spring Hill.
Hughes, C. (2010) *Urban Beekeeping*. The Good Life Press.

Cheese
Ash, R. (2009) *Self Sufficiency Cheesemaking*. New Holland Publishers.
Peacock, P. (2010) *Making Your Own Cheese*. Spring Hill.

Chickens
Beeken, L. (2010) *Chicken Manual: The Complete Step-by-Step Guide to Keeping Chickens*. J. H. Haynes & Co.
Shirt, V. (2007) *The Right Way to Keep Chickens*. Elliot Right Way Books.

Chicken coops
Brock, T. et al. (2010) *Building Chicken Coops for Dummies*. John Wiley and Sons.

Cider and mead

Pooley, M. and Lomax, J. (1999) *Real Cider Making on a Small Scale*. Special Interest Model Books.

Schramm, K. (2003) *Compleat Meadmaker: Home Production of Honey Wine for Your First Batch to Award-Winning Fruit and Herb Variations*. Brewers Publications (an American book, but very useful for the UK).

Dyeing

Dean, J. (2010) *Wild Colour: How to Grow, Prepare and Use Natural Plant Dyes*. Mitchell Beazley.

Lambert, E. (2010) *Complete Guide to Natural Dyeing*. Search Press.

Flowers

Byczynski, L. (1997) *The Flower Farmer*. Chelsea Green Publishing.

Raven, S. (1996) *The Cutting Garden: Growing and Arranging Garden Flowers*. Frances Lincoln.

Goats

Mowlem, A. (2001) *Practical Goatkeeping*. Crowood Press.

Weaver, S. (2006) *Goats: Small-Scale Goat Keeping for Pleasure and Profit*. Bow Tie Press.

Herbs

Brown, D. (2008) *RHS Encyclopedia of Herbs*. Dorling Kindersley.

McVicar, J. (2009) *Jekka's Complete Herb Book*. Kyle Cathie.

Preserves

Corbin, P. (2008) *Preserves: River Cottage Handbook No. 2*. Bloomsbury Press.
Prince, T. (2008) *Jams and Chutneys: Preserving the Harvest*. Dorling Kindersley.

Soaps

Ade, S. (2009) *Soap Making*. New Holland Publishers.
Miller Cavitch, S. (1995) *The Natural Soap Book: Making Herbal and Vegetable-Based Soaps*. Storey Publishing.

Soft fruits

Baker, H. (1999) *RHS Encyclopedia of Practical Gardening: Growing Fruit*. Octopus Publishing Group.
Eastoe, J. (2007) *Home-grown Fruit*. Collins and Brown.

USEFUL ADDRESSES AND WEBSITES

Rules and regulations

Environmental Health: Contact your local government office and they will put you through to the correct department. Alternatively, put 'Environmental Health' and your town in an internet search engine and a relevant website will come up.

Food Standards Agency: www.food.gov.uk

HM Revenue and Customs: www.hmrc.gov.uk
0845 9154515

Legislation: www.legislation.gov.uk
Official government website dealing with all aspects of legislation.

Trading Standards Institute: www.tradingstandards.gov.uk
0845 4040506

Business support and advice

Business Link: www.businesslink.gov.uk
0845 6009006

Business Connect Wales: www.startups.co.uk/business-connect-wales

Business Gateway (for businesses in Scotland): www.bgateway.com
0845 6096611

DEFRA (Department for Environment, Food and Rural Affairs): www.defra.gov.uk
0845 9335577

Federation of Small Businesses: www.fsb.org.uk
01253 336000

National Farmers' Union: www.nfuonline.com
024 7685 8500

WiRE (Women in Rural Enterprise): www.wireuk.org
01952 815338

Markets

Country Markets Ltd: www.country-markets.co.uk

FARMA (National Farmers' Retail and Markets Association): www.farma.org.uk

Farmers' Markets: www.farmersmarkets.net
0845 4588420

Bees

Crossmoor Honey Farm: www.crossmoorhoney.com
Keeps Barn Farm, Crossmoor, Preston, Lancashire PR4 3XB
Bees, hive equipment and honey.

British Beekeepers' Association: www.britishbee.org.uk
National Beekeeping Centre, National Agricultural Centre, Stoneleigh, Warwickshire CV8 2LZ

Cheese

Gill Pateman, Merlin Cheeses: www.merlincheeses.co.uk
Tyn-y-Llwyn, Pontrhydygroes, Ystrad Meurig, Ceredigion SY25 6DP
01974 282636
Email: enquiries@merlincheeses.co.uk
Cheese maker operating a mail order service.

Specialist Cheesemakers Association: www.specialistcheesemakers.co.uk
17 Clerkenwell Green, London EC1R 0DP
020 7253 2114
Email: info@specialistcheesemakers.co.uk

Chickens

www.chickenbreeds.info
www.chickenkeepers.co.uk

Chicken coops

www.chickenkeepers.co.uk

Cider and mead
National Association of Cider Makers: www.cideruk.com
C/o Gemma Keyes, Secretary, NACM, International Wine and Spirit Centre, 39–45 Bermondsey Street, London SE1 3XF
Email: gemma@cideruk.com

Dyeing
Teresinha Roberts: www.wildcolours.co.uk
Unit I-135, The Custard Factory, Gibb Street, Birmingham B9 4AA
Email: info@wildcolours.co.uk
Dyestuff and equipment via the internet and mail order.

The Association of Guilds of Weavers, Spinners and Dyers:
www.wsd.org.uk
Email: secretary@wsd.org.uk

Flowers
Andrea Jones, Mayfield Flowers: www.mayfieldflowers.co.uk
12 Fenwick Road, Kilmaurs, Ayrshire KA3 2TD
01563 543585, 07973 257190
Seasonal cut flower grower.

Royal Horticultural Society: www.rhs.org.uk
80 Vincent Square, London SW1P 2PE
Information on all aspects of growing.

Goats
Gill and Martin McManoman
Marimar, Cumeragh Lane, Whittingham, Preston, Lancashire PR3 2AN
01772 860856
Goat products, available at markets in the northwest of England.

British Goat Society: www.allgoats.com
01434 240866
Email: secretary@allgoats.com

Herbs

Jekka's Herb Farm: www.jekkasherbfarm.com
Rose Cottage, Shellards Lane, Alveston, Bristol BS35 3SY
Organic herb grower operating mail order and online sales.

Herb Society: www.herbsociety.org.uk
Sulgrave Manor, Sulgrave, Banbury, Oxfordshire OX17 2SD

Preserves

Susan Carvell
32 Hugh Barn Lane, New Longton, Preston, Lancashire PR4 4XA
07815 491805
Handmade traditional cakes and preserves.

Guild of Jam and Preserve Makers: www.jamguild.com
PO Box 2979, Bristol BS5 5EY
Email: info@jamguild.com

Soaps

Linda Clough, Pura Soaps: www.purasoaps.com
01282 703313
Email: purasoaps@gmail.com
Handmade soaps via the internet and mail order.

Guild of Craft Soap and Toiletry Makers: www.gcstm.co.uk
Suite 306, Kemp House, 152–160 City Road, London EC1V 2NX
Email: info@gcstm.co.uk

Soft fruits

Royal Horticultural Society: www.rhs.org.uk
80 Vincent Square, London SW1P 2PE
Information on all aspects of growing.

INDEX